THE
WEEKEND
DECORATOR

THE
WEEKEND
DECORATOR

GINA MOORE
AMY DAWSON

A Dorling Kindersley Book

INTRODUCTION

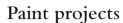

With the fast pace of life today there never seems to be the time to make those home improvements which feel so necessary. Yet as *The Weekend Decorator* shows, furniture, windows, even a whole room can be transformed in just a weekend, if not a few hours.

The time-conscious projects are also stylish and require no special skills. The step-by-step instructions will guide you through the projects and any further information you will need is explained and illustrated in the chapters on basic techniques.

Each project has a guide to the time it will take at the top of the page, so that you will know at a glance how many hours to set aside for it. The time given is the actual time needed for working on the project. It assumes that you have done any necessary preparation such as taking measurements for calculating curtain fabric or preparing a wall for painting, and organised all materials and bought the fabric, paint or other items needed. Each project starts with an itemised list of tools and materials. Make sure you have all to hand before you start – otherwise you may find yourself stuck half way through a project with a vital piece of material missing.

Paint projects

One of the easiest ways to transform a room is to give it a coat of paint. Paint is cheap, easy to obtain and straighforward to apply. A simple colourwash can give a room a whole new personality. With a little more effort you can achieve exciting effects, such as stencilling, stamping or trompe l'oeil panels. Alternatively, try some of the furnishing projects. Transform your kitchen cupboard doors with a Shaker-look dragged effect or paint some old frames with crackle glaze. A junk shop find can become a gleaming lacquered cupboard or an old garden chair be given a new lease of life with a verdigris effect.

Thorough preparation

For the best results, always prepare thoroughly before starting a project. When short of time it may be tempting to cut corners, but you will always regret it and rushing may cost time in the end. Make sure walls are clean and free of grease and dust before you start. Fill any cracks and sand down any rough patches. Clear the room of as much furniture as possible and cover any items that cannot be moved. If you are doing a project with a design such as stripes or checks, measure the area carefully first to check how well the design fits your wall and adapt if necessary. Furniture, whether new or old, should be stripped of paint if necessary and always sanded and wiped clean to provide a good, even surface for the paint to adhere to.

If you are trying a special paint effect such as stippling or stencilling for the first time, experiment first on some lining paper and practice the technique until you feel confident. Choose your paint colours carefully. Many manufacturers now supply sample pots you can take home and try out before making up your mind. Be sure to buy enough paint for the job as different batches won't always match. Most

manufacturers provide guidelines on the tin. If you mix glazes yourself, keep note of the different colours and quantities you use in case more has to be mixed.

Fabric projects

If you feel like working with fabric rather than paint, the soft furnishing projects in this book can be used to add colour, comfort and a dash of style to every room in your home. You may choose to frame your windows with elegant curtains, or more simply with a classic blind. You may be inspired to transform your bedroom with a dramatic canopy, or revamp a bedhead with a padded cover. There are quilts, cushions, and storage solutions from which to draw inspiration and, with a little thought, all of them can be adapted to suit your own particular needs.

First, choose your fabric.

You will find that there is a vast array available and it is important to take time when making your selection to ensure the fabric is right for the room and the project. Ask for sample swatches of the fabrics that catch your eye. Take them home and look at them in situ, both in daylight and artificial light. Look at the colour and pattern and try to imagine the impact, either subtle or daring, the fabrics would have on your room. Consider their weight, texture and the way they behave – do they drape beautifully for a curtain or throw? Does the feel of the fabric lend itself to a cushion or quilt? Will it be strong enough for a loose cover? Finally you should think about aftercare: will the fabric shrink when washed, or will the colours fade?

Take care to measure and estimate properly. Study the instructions in the techniques section on measuring and estimating fabric. Read the guidelines for the particular project you are going to do thoroughly before you start. There is nothing worse than clearing the decks for a weekend of creative endeavour, only to find out that you have underestimated the amount of fabric you need. When in doubt, buy more than you think you need – any leftover fabric can be used to trim another project!

Be inspired

Remember that all the projects in this book are essentially quick and simple and well within your capabilities, however much you doubt them. You don't need any special skills so don't let yourself be put off. Clear a space to work and begin. You will be amazed at how enjoyably your weekend will pass. At the end, you will look on your handiwork with pride – and start to plan your next weekend project!

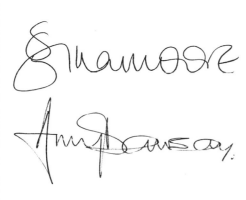

TIME GUIDE

2 HOURS

The clock face which appears in every project gives a guide to the length of time it will take to complete the work. Painting walls and floors will vary depending on the size of the room - the time given is for a 3 x 3.6m (10 x 12ft) wall or floor.

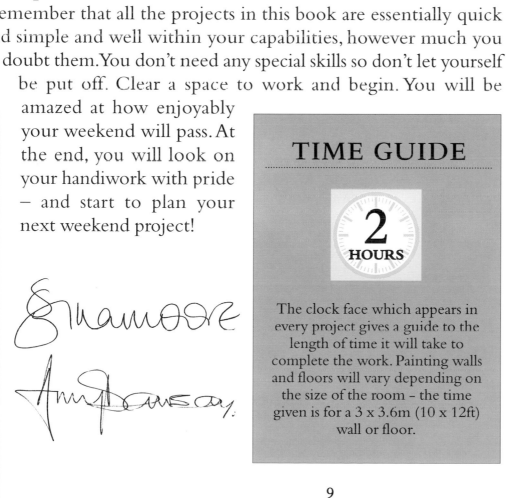

9

Hallways

STONE BLOCKS

Dramatic effect • Adds texture • Creates grandeur

PAINTED STONE blocks give a cool airy feeling and help to create an illusion of space in a room. They look their best in an area such as a hallway, where there is usually a minimum of furniture and clutter to conflict with their clean lines. The wall is first colourwashed in a creamy yellow shade and the brush marks softened with a dry brush. Once you have worked out the size of the blocks these are marked on the wall in pencil. Finally, the pencil lines are carefully painted over with brown acrylic paint and highlighted in white.

Cool sophistication *A look of cool sophistication is brought to this hall by the use of painted stone blocks. The colourwash ground gives an impression of texture, while the lines break up a long wall.*

PROJECT PLANNER

3½ HOURS

Tools and Materials

Cream or pale yellow vinyl matt emulsion • Ready-mixed buff or creamy-yellow colourwash or mix your own with raw umber artist's acrylic and scumble glaze (see p.165) • Raw umber artist's acrylic • White artist's acrylic • Roller and tray • Paintbrush • Small artist's brush • Softening brush • Mutton cloth • Ruler • Pencil • Spirit level

2 Take the ready-mixed colourwash or mix your own (see p.165). Working in sections (see p.170), start to apply the colourwash with the paintbrush. Use rough criss-crossing strokes and allow the coverage to be lighter in some places, not too even.

1 Prepare the wall (see p.169). Using a roller, apply a coat of cream or pale yellow vinyl matt emulsion. The yellower the colour of this base, the warmer the stone effect will look. Leave to dry for 30 minutes.

3 While the paint on the first section of wall is still wet, take a piece of mutton cloth, bunch it up in your hand and lightly dab over the wall, softening and lifting the paint. This removes some of the bigger brush strokes.

4 Then take a dry softening brush and brush over the area to soften the brush marks further. Repeat Steps 2 to 4 until the wall is complete.

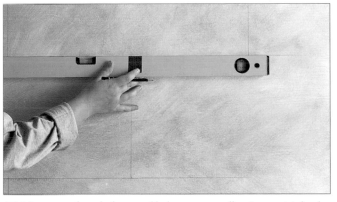

5 Measure and mark the stone blocks on your wall, using a spirit level to check that lines are straight. The rows should be staggered as in a real stone wall. (See p.176 for more information on measuring and marking stone blocks). The blocks here measure 30 x 60cm (12 x 24in).

6 Mix some raw umber acrylic paint with a small amount of white acrylic to soften it slightly. Using a small artist's brush, carefully hand paint over the pencil lines marking the blocks. Start from the top and work down.

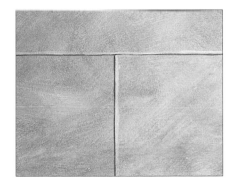

7 Using white acrylic, highlight the brown lines. Work to the right of vertical lines and above horizontal lines. The white lines do not have to go right along each line – they look best if slightly broken and uneven.

BLIND WITH TIES

Sculptural simplicity • Makes a decorative screen • No complicated cording system

DECORATIVE RATHER than functional, this blind is most suitable for a hall or stairway window, where there is no need for it to be raised too often. It looks its best when at least half lowered and makes a useful screen for an unappealing view, such as a busy street or an ugly brick wall. The fabric is unlined to allow maximum light through when lowered.

The blind is simply slotted onto a pole. This should extend at least 15cm (6in) either side of the window frame, since the ties will pull the fabric slightly inwards. Allow at least 20cm (8in) extra in the length of the blind to give the pleats fullness even when the blind is lowered.

Choose a fabric that is light but has enough body to hold the shape of the blind. The example here is made from a closely woven mercerised cotton, with a slightly stiff texture. A silk taffeta or shantung would also be a good choice, although silk should always be lined. Consider using a bold pattern – since so much flat fabric is on display, any design is shown off to full advantage. The ties here have been cut across the width of the fabric for contrast.

Graceful pleats

This blind's sculptural beauty lies in its simplicity. There is no complicated cording system and the fabric is simply pleated up by hand and held in place with loosely knotted ties. The fabric then falls gracefully at each side. To lower the blind completely, simply undo the ties and allow it to fall to its full length. Here the ties have been made from the same fabric as the blind, but a plain or contrasting fabric could also be used.

PROJECT PLANNER

2 HOURS

Tools and Materials

Main fabric: length of window plus 10cm (4in) for slot at top plus 2cm (¾in) for base hem and 20cm (8in) for fullness x width of window plus 15cm (6in) either side and 4cm (1½in) for side hems (see p.129 for information on measuring windows) • Two straight ties (see p.146) each with a finished width of 5cm (2in) x twice the length of blind • Curtain pole • Sewing machine and thread to match fabric

1 *Press and pin 1cm (⅜in) double hems at both sides and base of the blind. Machine stitch hems in place.*

2 *At the top of the blind, press over 1cm (⅜in) then 9cm (3½in) and pin in place. This forms the slot for the pole.*

4 *Machine stitch the ties in place on the fold line, backstitching at the start and finish to secure.*

3 *Make ties (see p.146). Place fabric right side up on the table, opening out the 9cm (3½in) fold at the top. Take one tie and mark the centre point of its length. Place the tie about 30cm (12in) from the side edge of the blind with the centre point on the pressed fold line and pin. Position second tie 30cm (12in) from other side of the blind in the same way.*

5 *Place the blind wrong side up and re-fold the top to form the slot for the pole. Pin and machine stitch close to the folded edge, making sure that the ties are well out of the way and do not get caught in the stitching. Once the blind has been put up, check the length of the ties, trim if necessary and finish ends by hand.*

CONTRAST-LINED DOOR CURTAIN

Keeps out draughts • Looks warm and welcoming • Brightens two rooms

A DOOR CURTAIN can serve as a draught excluder and helps to give a welcoming look to a hall. Here an embroidered natural linen fabric makes an elegantly muted statement while the flamboyant red check on the reverse presents an entirely different face to the adjoining room. The heading is unstiffened in keeping with the relaxed nature of the curtain. A fabric tie-back, attached to a hook by the doorway, holds the curtain back for access. If there is room to the side of the door, use a wider pole so that the curtain can be pulled right out of the way if necessary.

Elegant door curtain *Look for fabrics that work well together, not only in pattern and colour, but also in weight. A flimsy fabric would sag and pull if teamed with a much weightier material.*

PROJECT PLANNER

Tools and Materials

3 HOURS

Main fabric: length of door plus 4cm (1½in) for base hem and 10cm (4in) for top hem x twice the width of pole, plus 4cm (1½in) for side seam allowances, joining widths if necessary (see p.129) • Contrast fabric: as main fabric • Tie-back (see p.149): cut one 20 x 80cm (8 x 31½in) in either fabric • Curtain hooks, one for every 10cm (4in) of fabric and one for each end • Curtain pole and rings (same number as hooks) • Sewing machine and thread to match fabric

1 Place main fabric and contrast fabric right sides together and pin at the sides, leaving a 2cm (¾in) seam allowance. Machine stitch side seams, leaving the bottom 7.5cm (3in) of the fabric open.

2 Turn the curtain the right way out. At the bottom, turn in 4cm (1½in) hems on both lengths of fabric to the inside of the curtain. Press and pin in place.

3 Using even slipstitch (see p.138), sew the folded edges at the base of the curtain together, making sure you finish the open edges above the corners at each side.

4 Turn over a double 5cm (2in) hem at the top of the curtain, folding the main fabric over the contrast fabric. Press

5 Work out how many curtain hooks you need. Allow one for each end and arrange the rest at even intervals roughly 10cm (4in) apart across the curtain top. Using couching stitch (see p.139), attach each hook 12mm (½in) below the curtain top. Attach each hook firmly, adding a few stitches at the top to keep it from flopping forward (see p.139).

6 Make a stiffened tie-back (see p.149), with a finished width of 9cm (3½in). Stitch a ring to each end on the wrong side to attach the tie to a hook on the wall to hold the curtain back.

CONSOLE TABLE COVER

Conceals an old table • Elegant and practical • Provides hidden storage area

WITH A SMART full-length fabric cover, a basic table or shelf system in the hall becomes not only a useful surface but also provides a concealed storage area underneath. If you do not have a table of a suitable size for your hall, a simple structure can be constructed from blockboard. It is important to take measurements very carefully and to allow 5mm to 1cm (¼in to ⅜in) ease to every dimension when you cut out your fabric panels. If the cover fits the table too tightly, it will not hang well at the corners.

A simple shape *The skirts of the cover are split at the front corners and are held in place with fabric ties. Use upholstery-weight fabrics with enough body to hang well over such a simple shape.*

PROJECT PLANNER

2½ HOURS

Tools and Materials

Main fabric: measure the table. Cut two panels the width and height of the table, plus 4cm (¾in) seam allowance all round; cut two side panels the depth and height of the table, plus 4cm (¾in) seam allowance all round; cut one top panel to fit the top, plus 4cm (1½in) seam allowance
- Ties: cut 8 bias strips to make ties with a finished width of 2 x 25cm (¾ x10in) (see p.148)
- Sewing machine and thread to match or contrast with fabric

1 Place a side panel and front panel right sides together, aligning them at the top edges, and pin. Taking a 2cm (¾in) seam allowance, machine stitch down to 12.5cm (5in) from the top. Backstitch to secure stitching firmly. Repeat to attach the remaining side panel to the other edge of the front panel. Attach the back panel to the free edges of the side panels, stitching all the way down to the base hem.

2 Press the seams open. Press under double 1cm (⅜in) hems along the raw edges at the front and around the bottom hem.

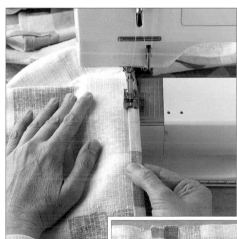

4 Pin the top panel to the skirt, leaving a 2cm (¾in) seam allowance. When you get to a corner, snip into the seam allowance so you can separate the edges to make a right angle (see p.136). Leaving the needle in the work, lift the foot and pivot the work. Lower the foot again and continue stitching down next side.

3 Machine stitch all round double side hems and the base hem. When you reach the seam, lift the foot, turn the work, lower the foot and stitch across the seam. Repeat to turn the work again and continue stitching down the other side. Snip into the seam allowance just above the stitching so that the seam lies flat (see inset).

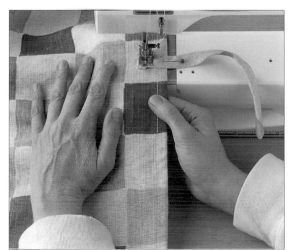

5 Make 8 bias ties (see p.148). Finish one end of each tie. Tucking the unfinished end under, pin a tie to the right side of the front panel about one third of the way down from the top and 2.5cm (1in) in from the line of machine stitching. Machine stitch in place (see p.146). Stitch a second tie two-thirds of the way down from the top. Stitch matching ties to the adjoining panel. Repeat to stitch ties at the other side of the front panel.

LIVING ROOMS

PEARLY STRIPES

Cool contemporary style • Easily achieved elegance • Adds a glamorous touch

PEARLY PAINT lends an instant touch of glamour and style to any room. Try painting a room in these stripes or decorate just one wall for a more subtle look. The wall is painted in the base colour first and the stripes are then measured and marked out. Every other stripe is masked off and painted in the pearly finish, leaving the stripes in between in the base colour.

Always use low-tack masking tape for masking off stripes like these or you are in danger of pulling off paint when you remove the tape.

An elegant sheen *The lustrous sheen of these pearly stripes makes a perfect backdrop to modern furnishings and brings light and vivacity to your living room.*

PROJECT PLANNER

4¼ HOURS

Tools and Materials
Vinyl matt emulsion in base colour • Pearly metallic paint in stripe colour • Paintbrush • Mini-roller • Low-tack masking tape • Pencil • Ruler • Spirit level

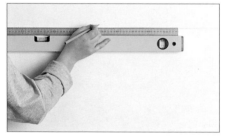

1 *Prepare the wall (see p.169) and apply vinyl matt emulsion in the base colour all over the area (see p.166). Leave to dry for about 30 minutes.*

2 *Measure the wall and divide into horizontal stripes (see p.175). The stripes here are 20cm (8in) wide. Mark the stripes lightly in pencil, using a spirit level to make sure they are straight.*

3 *Using low-tack masking tape, mask alternate stripes to be painted in the metallic colour. Place the tape very carefully along the outside edges of the stripes to be painted in metallic paint. (The stripes in between remain in the base colour.)*

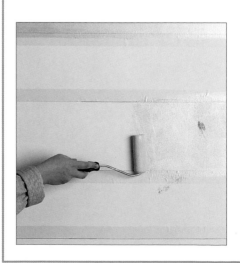

4 *Using a mini-roller, apply a coat of metallic paint to the masked stripes. Make sure you work right up to the masking tape and allow paint to go over the tape. Leave this first coat to dry thoroughly for 30 minutes and apply a second coat.*

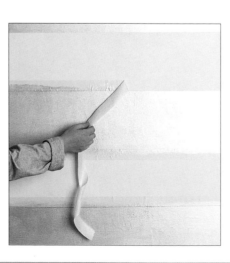

5 *When the stripes are complete, gently peel off the masking tape.*

ENVELOPE CUSHIONS

Add comfort and colour • Quick and simple to make • Range of finishes

CUSHIONS GIVE an instant dash of personality to a room, adding colour, texture and a welcoming touch. The simple envelope cover is like a housewife pillowcase and is made from one length of fabric folded to form a pocket, with an inside flap that holds the cushion pad in place. Once you have mastered this simple construction, vary the covers by making the length of fabric out of separate pieces, so that the main cover and flap are different colours, and by adding finishing touches such as buttons and ties to hold the cover closed.

Coordinating cushions *Pick fabrics that reflect the simple nature of the covers, such as plain linens and silks or checked or striped cottons. Choose a range of two or three colours that work well together.*

PROJECT PLANNER

3 HOURS

Tools and Materials

Three cushion pads 45 x 45cm (18 x 18in) • Fabric for one of each cushion (covers should fit snugly so do not add seam allowances): three main panels 45 x 90cm (18 x 36in); three contrast flaps 45 x 20cm (18 x 8in); one contrast strip 45 x 9cm (18 x 3½in) • Fabric for two straight ties (see p.146) with a finished size of 4 x 25cm (1½ x 4in) • Three buttons • Length of iron-on interfacing 7 x 45cm (2¾ x 18in) • Sewing machine and thread to match fabric

Envelope cushion

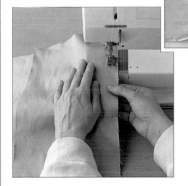

1 Place the contrast flap along the top edge of the main panel, right sides together, and pin. Machine stitch 1.5cm (⅝ in) from the raw edges. Press. Press over a 1cm (⅜ in) double hem at each end of the cover and pin. Machine stitch in place (see inset).

2 Fold the main panel in half and fold the contrast flap down over the main panel. Pin the side seams together. Machine stitch 1.5cm (⅝ in) from the raw edges, starting at the top of the contrast panel. Turn the cover right side out.

Envelope cushion with ties

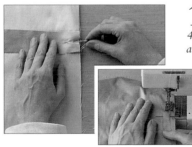

1 Make two straight ties (see p.146), each measuring 4 x 25cm (1½ x 4in). Place one at the centre of the right side at the top of the main panel. Place contrast flap right side down over the tie and pin in place. Machine stitch the contrast flap to main panel, stitching over the tie (see inset).

2 Press over a 1cm (⅜ in) double hem at each end of the cover and pin. Machine stitch in place. Pin the second tie to the centre of the other end of the cover. Stitch round in a rectangle to attach the tie (see p.146). Fold the main panel in half so that the base aligns with the seam of the top edge and contrast flap. Fold the contrast flap down over the main panel. Finish as in Step 2 of the envelope cushion.

Envelope cushion with buttons

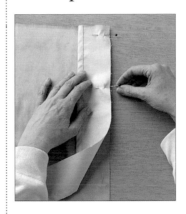

1 Take the strip of contrast fabric measuring 45 x 9cm (18 x 3½in) and attach iron-on interfacing to the wrong side, following maker's instructions. Turn over a 1cm (⅜in) double hem along one side, pin and machine. Place the strip along one end of the main panel, right sides together, and pin. Machine stitch, taking a 1cm (⅜in) seam allowance.

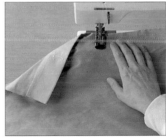

2 Working from the right side of the cover with the interfaced strip underneath, mark the position of the buttonholes. Position one in the centre and one 12.5cm (5in) each side of the centre. Stitch the buttonholes by machine (see p.152).

3 Take a flap of contrast fabric 45 x 20cm (18 x 8in) and fold in half with wrong sides together. Stitch the folded fabric to the right side of the other end of the cover.

4 Fold the cover and stitch the side seams as in Step 2 of the envelope cushion. Turn the cover right side out and sew the buttons onto the contrast flap.

31

CUBE FOOTSTOOL

Versatile and practical • Inexpensive yet stylish • Quick to make

THIS UP-TO-DATE version of the footstool is simply a sleek foam cube, covered with a smooth-textured, suede-effect fabric. It doubles as a seat and occasional table, too. Use the firmest grade of upholstery foam available. If you cannot get the thickness required, ask your supplier to bond layers of foam together to the required depth. Two sizes are shown – a perfect cube and a

slightly taller version. Check that the fabric you choose has been treated with Scotchgard™ or use a spray-on fabric protector to provide some protection from dirt and spills.

A minimalist shape *Select a strong, upholstery-grade fabric to cover the cube. Suede and leather-effect fabrics lend themselves to this minimalist shape, but corduroys and tweeds would also look good.*

PROJECT PLANNER

2 HOURS

Tools and Materials
Foam cube measuring 40 x 40 x 40cm (16 x 16 x 16in) • Stockinette to cover (see p.155) • Piece of wadding 40 x 40cm (16 x 16in) • Fabric: cut four panels for the sides, each 40 x 40cm (16 x 16in) plus 1.5cm (⅝in) seam allowance all round, plus two panels for the top and bottom, each 40 x 40cm (16 x 16in) plus 1.5cm (⅝in) seam allowance all round • Sewing machine and thread to match fabric

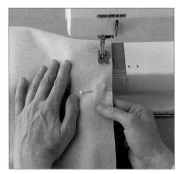

1 *Pin side panels, wrong sides together, taking a 1.5cm (⅝in) seam allowance. Machine stitch.*

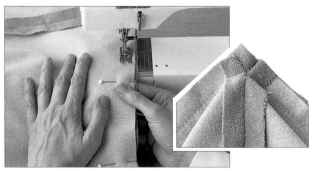

2 *Pin the top edges of all four side panels to the top panel, wrong sides together. Machine stitch. As you near a corner, snip into the side panel seam to fit round the corner (see p.136). At the corner, leave the needle in the work, lift foot and pivot work. Lower the foot and continue stitching along top of next side panel (see inset).*

3 *When the stitching is complete, snip across each corner, taking care not to cut the stitching. This helps to reduce bulk and ensure that the cover fits neatly.*

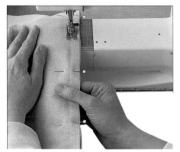

4 *Pin and machine the base panel to the bottom of one side panel, taking a 1.5cm (⅝in) seam allowance.*

5 *Press over a 1.5cm (⅝in) seam allowance on the remaining three sides of the base panel and on the free edges of the side panels.*

6 *Place the wadding on top of the cube and cover the cube with stockinette (see p.155). Push the cube into the cover. Using a double length of thread, sew the open side with even slipstitch (see p.138).*

THROW

Coordinates your colour scheme • Adds texture and variation • Warm and cosy

A THROW IS AN extremely useful decorating device – a clever choice of fabric or colour can help to tie together disparate elements of a decorating scheme. Use a throw to introduce a touch of contrast colour to enliven a monochrome scheme or add an element of soft and contrasting texture to a hard-surfaced room. By finishing the throw with lavish trimmings you can create instant style and luxury. But, don't forget that on a chilly evening, a throw's primary function is to provide extra warmth and comfort. The throw shown here is made with two layers of soft and textured chenille in up-to-the-minute colours, trimmed with a chunky bullion fringe.

Draping fabrics *Choose fabrics that drape beautifully and feel good to the touch. Don't forget to look at dress fabrics as well, but avoid fabrics that crease easily such as linen or crisp cottons.*

PROJECT PLANNER

2½ HOURS

Tools and Materials
For a throw measuring 1.5 x 1.2m (5 x 4ft), cut two pieces of fabric to this size, plus 2cm (¾in) seam allowances • 2.5m (2¾yd) fringing • Masking tape • Sewing machine and thread to match fabric

1 *Cut the length of fringing in half – one half for each short side of the fabric. Put a piece of masking tape at each end of the fringe to stop it fraying. Place one piece of fabric right side up and pin a length of fringe to each short side. Tack (see p.138) to hold it in place.*

2 *Place the other panel of fabric right side down on top of fringed fabric. Tack all round, leaving a large opening at the centre of one long side. Take care to stitch at the base of the welt of the fringing and to stitch through all layers. At the corners stitch between the fringe tassels.*

3 *Machine stitch all round, except for the opening, following the line of tacking and making sure you stitch through all layers. At the corners take a couple of stitches across the corner before pivoting the fabric and stitching down the next side (see blunting corners p.136).*

4 *Cut across each corner of the throw, trimming off the protruding tassels.*

5 *Remove tacking stitches and turn the throw the right way out. Tuck in the raw edges at the opening and pin. Hand sew the folded edges together using even slipstitch (see p.138).*

ROMAN BLIND

A simplified version • Neat and economical • Easy to hang

A ROMAN BLIND makes economical use of fabric and space and is a useful covering for windows with little room at either side for curtains. This simplified version has only one rod and rod pocket and is rather less tailored and severe than the normal design. Fabrics should be lightweight and soft rather than crisp – linens, muslins or Indian cotton are all suitable. The blind is attached with velcro to a covered lath. The lath can be screwed directly into the recess of the window, or fixed to the window frame or the wall above with right-angled brackets.

A simple look *Emphasise the blind's simplicity by choosing a plain fabric or graphic patterns, such as stripes, checks or a single repeating motif, which will not be lost when the blind is raised.*

PROJECT PLANNER

3 HOURS

Tools and Materials

Main fabric: finished length plus 23cm (9in) hem allowances x finished width plus 10cm (4in) side seam allowances; (see p.129 for information on measuring window) • Lining: finished length, less 15cm (6in), plus 2cm (¾in) seam allowances x finished width, less 4cm (1½in) • Velcro to fit finished width • Dowel rod to fit finished width • Rings for cording the back of the blind (see p.145) • Tailor's chalk • Sewing machine and thread to match fabric

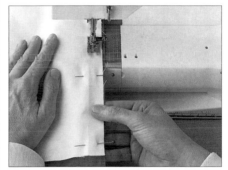

1 Place main fabric and lining right sides together, aligning top edges. Pin and machine side seams, taking a 1.5cm (⅝in) seam allowance.

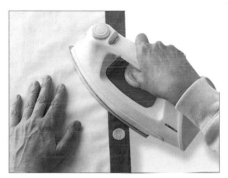

2 Turn right side out and centre the lining so that it is about 3.5cm (1½in) in from each side. Press along each side.

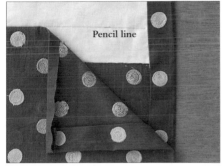

Pencil line

3 Draw a pencil line across the bottom of the lining 5cm (2in) up from the bottom edge. Turn a 1cm (⅜in) hem up along bottom of main fabric and press. Fold main fabric up to meet the pencil line. Press and pin in place.

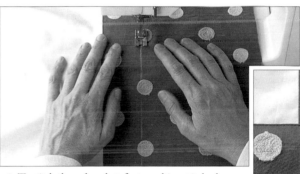

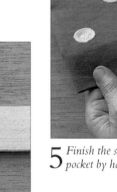

4 To stitch the rod pocket, first machine stitch along the top folded edge of the main fabric. Using tailor's chalk, mark a line 5cm (2in) below this. Machine stitch along the chalk line. Insert the rod into the finished pocket (see inset).

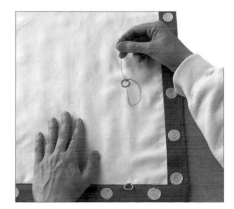

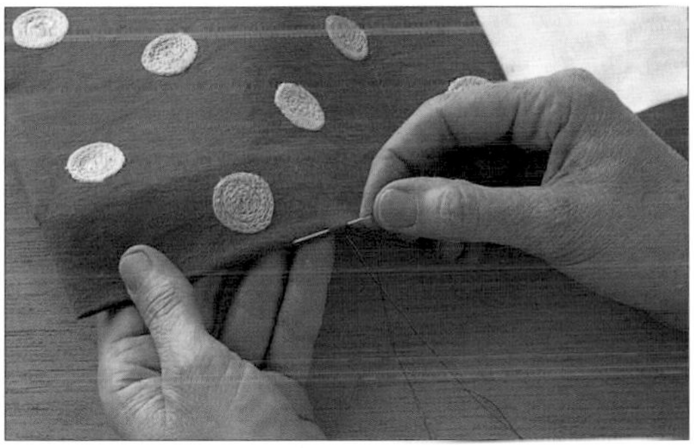

5 Finish the sides of the rod pocket and seams below the pocket by hand, using even slipstitch (see p.138).

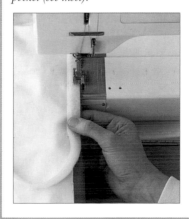

6 Fold over 2cm (¾in) at top edge of blind. Pin and press. Attach the velcro strip (soft side), machine stitching at the top and bottom of the strip.

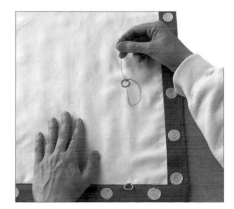

7 Attach the rings for cording the blind. Using couching stitch (see p.139) sew one ring 10cm (4in) in from the edge of the blind at the top of the rod pocket. Stitch another in the centre and a third 10cm (4in) from the other side of the blind. Stitch the next row 20cm (8in) above the first (see p.145 for more information on cording). Make sure you attach the rings through all layers of fabric. Fix the blind to a covered lath (see p.144).

CRACKLE FRAMES

Unites assorted frames • Coordinates with pictures • Makes dull frames special

CRACKLE GLAZE simulates the effect of old paint that has cracked and peeled slightly to reveal another layer underneath. It can be used to rejuvenate an old battered frame or make a cheap wooden frame something special. Crackle glaze also helps to coordinate a group of different frames and give them a pleasingly aged look. Choose colours to work with your room or with the pictures to be framed. The technique is very simple. Two different colours of vinyl matt emulsion are used. A coat of crackle glaze is applied over the first coat of paint and left to dry. When the second colour is applied the glaze causes it to crack slightly as it dries, revealing the first colour beneath. Crackle glaze could also be used on other small items such as boxes and lamp bases.

Pleasing harmony

A collection of frames is given a pleasing harmony with crackle glaze. If working on several items, try changing the order in which you apply the two colours for a varied yet coordinated effect.

PROJECT PLANNER

Tools and Materials
Two contrasting colours of vinyl matt emulsion • Crackle glaze • Varnish (matt, satin or gloss) • Paintbrushes • Brush for varnishing • Sandpaper

5¾ HOURS

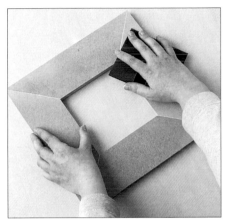

1 *Sand down the frame carefully, removing any rough or uneven areas.*

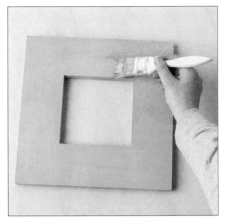

2 *Apply a coat of one colour of vinyl matt emulsion to the frame. Allow to dry for about 30 minutes.*

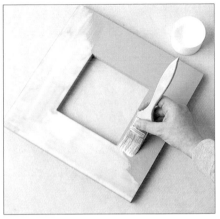

3 *Take the crackle glaze and apply to the frame. Work around the frame in one direction and make sure that the whole area is covered. Leave the glaze to dry for three hours.*

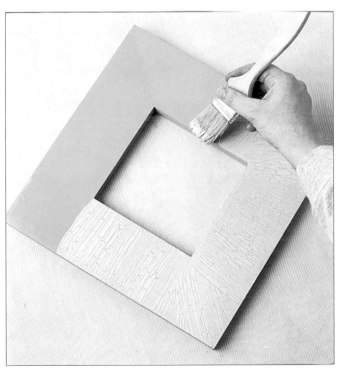

4 *Take the second colour of vinyl matt emulsion. Apply one coat, working across the frame at right angles to the direction of the glaze. Leave this coat to dry for an hour or until touch dry.*

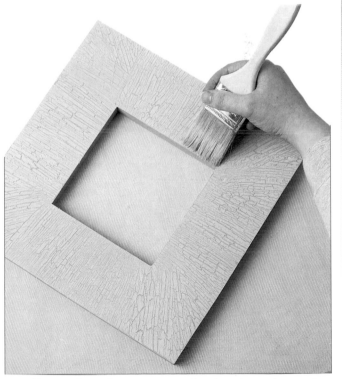

5 *Add a coat of varnish matt, satin or gloss depending on how much shine you want. Apply the varnish in the same direction as the second coat of paint (Step 4).*

PLEATED CURTAINS WITH PELMET

Simple but unusual design • Integral pelmet • Suits sheers and heavier fabrics

THE APPEAL OF these curtains lies in the horizontal pleats at the base and on the self-pelmet, which provide textural interest and shape. Ties made from bias-cut strips of the same fabric are inserted into the seam between the pelmet and the curtain, and then tied over the pole to hold the curtains in place. The style is perfect for dress curtains or sheers that are always drawn, but the curtains can be difficult to draw back and forth. If you need to open the curtains frequently, it may be best to tie them to curtain rings rather than directly onto the pole.

Choosing fabric *Select plain fabrics that speak for themselves, such as natural linens and fine cottons or the raw silk used here. This style would also suit sheer fabrics such as crisp voile or organza.*

PROJECT PLANNER

7 HOURS

Tools and Materials

Curtains: cut two, each measuring the finished drop, plus 4cm (1½in) seam allowances, plus 32cm (12½in) for pleats x 1½ times the width of window (see p.128) • Pelmet: cut two, each measuring 30cm (12in), plus 4cm (1½in) seam allowances, plus 16cm (6¼in) for pleats x 1½ times the width of window (see p.128) • Ties: 12 bias-cut ties (see p.148) with a finished width of 2.5cm (1in) and length of 50cm (20in) • Tailor's chalk • Sewing machine and thread to match fabric

1 *Fold in a 2cm (¾in) double hem along the base and sides of the curtain. Pin, press and machine stitch.*

2 *Using tailor's chalk and working on the right side of the curtain, draw a line across the curtain 10cm (4in) from the base. Draw another line 12cm (4¾in) above that, then two more at 12cm (4¾in) intervals.*

3 *Starting at top chalk line, press curtain over at each line, wrong sides together. Pin in place to form the pleats.*

4 *Machine stitch each pleat 4cm (1½in) above the fold line to hold it in place. To help you keep your stitching straight, stick a piece of masking tape on the machine bed as a guide (see p.135). To make the pelmet, repeat Steps 1 to 4 with the pelmet fabric, but marking only two lines, one 10cm (4in) from the base and one 12cm (4¾in) above that.*

5 *Make six bias ties for each curtain (see p.148). Fold each tie in half and pin the folded edge to the top of the wrong side of the curtain. Place one just in from each side and space the rest evenly across the width. (If your curtain is very wide you may need more than six ties.) With the right side of the pelmet face down, pin it to the top edge of the wrong side of the curtain (see inset).*

6 *Machine stitch the pelmet to the top of the curtain, stitching across the ties. Press the seam open and flip the pelmet to the right side of the curtain. Tie onto your curtain pole.*

DINING ROOMS

STAMPED WALLS

Simple wallpaper effect • Create your own design • Simple to do

THIS SIMPLE TECHNIQUE allows you to create the decorative look of wallpaper without the trouble. A wide range of wooden stamps is available that you can use to create your own individual design. The wall is first painted in your chosen base colour. Once you have measured the wall and worked out your design, mark the position of each stamp. Then you simply apply paint to the stamp and stamp the wall. Try to keep the stamps reasonably even although some slight variations in density will only add to the charm of this technique.

Simple shapes *Simple graphic shapes work best for this stamping technique. Keep them well spaced – if the shapes are too close together the wall will look too busy.*

PROJECT PLANNER

3 HOURS

Tools and Materials
Vinyl matt emulsion in two shades: one light, one dark • Wooden stamp • Small and large paintbrushes • Ruler • Pencil • Spirit level

1 *Prepare the wall (see p.169) and apply undercoat if necessary. Apply the lighter of your two shades of vinyl matt emulsion with a brush or roller (see p.166). Leave to dry.*

2 *Measure the wall and mark dots to help you position the stamp (see p.177). Each dot should mark the bottom left-hand corner of the stamp. The stamp here measures 10 x 10cm (4 x 4in) and there is 40cm (16in) between each stamp and 60cm (24in) between each horizontal row. Alternate rows should be staggered as shown. Use a spirit level to check your lines of dots are straight (see inset).*

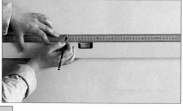

3 *Take the darker shade of vinyl matt emulsion and apply to the stamp with a small brush. Make sure the design is covered evenly and completely. There should be no lumps of excess paint.*

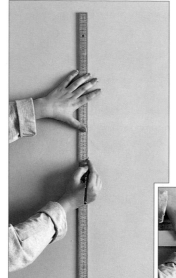

4 *Place the stamp on the wall, aligning the bottom left-hand corner with the dot. Roll the stamp forward, pressing hard to lay the paint – the curved base allows it to be rocked. Lift the stamp off the wall with one clean movement. It is a good idea to practice stamping on a piece of paper before starting on the wall.*

5 *Continue stamping until the wall is complete, reapplying paint each time to get stamps of a reasonably even density.*

1 Prepare
(see p. 16
remove any
coat of white
Leave to dr

4 M
u
water
water
almo
App
item
brus

5½
HOURS

COLOURWASH WALLS

Quick and easy • Adds texture to walls • Disguises rough walls

A RELAXED, INFORMAL effect, colourwashing brings some movement and texture to paintwork – a change from flat, even colour. It is also an excellent way of concealing uneven plastering. The wall is first painted with creamy emulsion. The glaze is then added in sections, using large, criss-crossing strokes, and brushed out with a dry badger brush while still wet. A ready-mixed colourwash can be used or you can make your own, using scumble glaze and your own combination of artist's acrylic colours (see p.165).

Timeless beauty *Warm and vibrant, a terracotta colourwash is an ideal background to minimalist furniture. The technique gives a feeling of age and timeless beauty to any interior.*

PROJECT PLANNER

1¾ HOURS

Tools and Materials
Cream vinyl matt emulsion • Terracotta colourwash (ready-mixed or see p.165 for instructions on mixing your own glaze) • Paint kettle • Paintbrush • Badger brush

1 *Prepare the wall (see p.169) and apply a coat of cream vinyl matt emulsion. The yellower the colour of the base coat, the warmer the final colourwash will be. Leave to dry.*

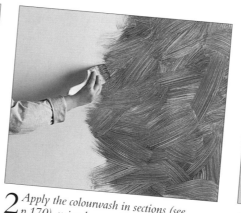

2 *Apply the colourwash in sections (see p.170), using large, criss-crossing strokes (see p.167). Take the brush down from the right to the left and then from the left down to the right with a flowing motion.*

3 *Take a dry badger brush and, while the glaze is still wet, soften the strokes on the area you have painted. Use criss-crossing strokes again, brushing first one way and then the other.*

4 *Apply colourwash to the next section as quickly as possible before the wet edge dries. Make sure this is carefully blended with the one before, leaving no white areas or hard lines.*

5 *Continue colourwashing and softening until the wall is covered. Pay particular attention to the joins between sections.*

TORTOISESHELL LAMP BASE

Rejuvenates an old lamp • Gives a sophisticated look • Simple to achieve

A TORTOISESHELL FINISH is not difficult to achieve and can be used to transform small items such as lamp bases, boxes and trays. As with all faux effects, study the real thing if you can before starting so you know the look you are aiming for.

The item is painted in warm yellow paint and then given a coat of wood stain. The side of a brush is used to make zigzag marks in the stain and some irregular lines are added in artist's acrylic paint. These are softened with a dry brush and the item is varnished to high gloss finish.

A luxurious look *Make an old wooden lamp base into something special with a luxurious tortoiseshell effect. Several different bases could be coordinated using this technique.*

PROJECT PLANNER

Tools and Materials

11 HOURS

Oil-based warm yellow paint • Mahogany wood stain
• Raw umber artist's oil paint • Black artist's oil paint
• White spirit • Gloss varnish • Paintbrushes • Small
artist's brush • Softening brush • Soft brush for varnishing

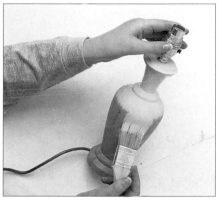

1 *If the lamp base is plain wood, you can paint straight on to it. If it already has a coat of paint, sand this down before starting. Apply a coat of oil-based warm yellow paint all over the lamp base and leave it to dry for one hour.*

2 *Apply a coat of mahogany wood stain over the whole lamp base.*

3 *While the stain is wet and using the side of the brush, make zigzag shapes in the stain all over the lamp base.*

4 *Using a little dark brown artist's oil paint and a small brush, add some small irregular lines over the surface.*

5 *Clean the brush with white spirit and repeat Step 4 with black oil paint, but make fewer, smaller lines and leave more space between them.*

6 *Take a clean, dry softening brush and lightly stroke it back and forth across the black and brown lines while they are still wet to soften them. Leave the lamp base to dry overnight.*

7 *Using gloss varnish and a soft brush, apply a coat of varnish to the lamp base and leave to dry thoroughly.*

GATHERED PELMET

Creates drama and atmosphere • Unusual design • Gives old curtains a new look

A PELMET OR VALANCE can make a dramatic statement over plain curtains and helps to give an illusion of height to a small window. Simple to make, the pelmet is gathered to its finished width and a strip of velcro is sewn over the gathers. It is then attached to a pelmet shelf that is fixed at the top of the window frame with right-angled shelf brackets. If there is room, the pelmet can be positioned above the window. When working out the width of the pelmet, remember that it must extend round the sides of the pelmet shelf (the returns) as well as across the front.

Contrasting stripes *Strips of black and cream fabric have been sewn together to make wide stripes and then finished with a shaped hem to create a softly gathered pelmet.*

PROJECT PLANNER

2½ HOURS

Tools and Materials

Fabric: panels of contrasting fabric, each panel measuring 18cm (7in) wide (including 3cm [1¼in] seam allowances) x 68cm (27in) long, to make a joined pelmet two and a half times the width of the pelmet shelf and returns • Lining fabric to fit joined panels, and an extra strip the finished width of the pelmet x 5.5cm (2¼in) • 2.5cm (1in) curtain tape • Velcro to fit finished width of pelmet • Cardboard for template • Tailor's chalk • Sewing machine and thread to match fabric

1 *Pin and machine stitch panels wrong sides together, taking 1.5cm (⅝ in) seam allowances, to make the required width of pelmet. Press the seams open.*

2 *Copy the template on p.179 onto a piece of card. Place the template on the wrong side of the fabric so that the points touch the bottom edge. Draw round the template with tailor's chalk. Lay the joined panels on the lining and pin, right sides together.*

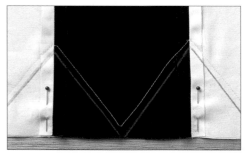

3 *Machine stitch panels and lining together, keeping the right-hand edge of the foot on the line. At a point, stop, lift the foot and pivot the work. Take one stitch across the point, lift the foot again and turn to go up the other side of the point.*

4 *Using a pair of sharp scissors, cut round the stitched shape, keeping about 5mm (¼in) away from the stitching. Snip off the ends of points (see inset).*

5 *Turn the pelmet the right side out. Using a pencil held inside the fabric, gently tease out the tip of each point. Press the pelmet carefully.*

6 *At the top of the pelmet, turn over 7.5cm (3in) to the lining side and press. Using tailor's chalk, mark a line 6cm (2½in) from the top. Pin the curtain tape in place with the top on the line. Machine stitch top and bottom (see p.141).*

7 *Pull up the cords on the curtain tape to gather the pelmet to the required width. Tie and finish the cords neatly (see p.141). Attach velcro (soft side) to the strip of lining fabric and stitch to the pelmet (see p.142). Prepare the pelmet shelf (see p.142), ready to hang your pelmet.*

KITCHENS

BENCH CUSHION

Comfortable and practical • Quick to make • Adds colour to your kitchen

THIS SIMPLE BOX cushion is ideal for use on a bench, banquette seating or window seat. Instead of having a separate box strip and piping, the cover is cut in one piece and sewn together like a flat cushion cover. Each corner is then squared off with a mitred seam.

To ring the changes, combine two coordinating fabrics and make another slip cover to tie over the first. This is a practical as well as attractive solution in a busy family kitchen – in the event of spills you can remove the outer slip cover to wash, while still leaving the main cover in place. The cushions used here have been made to measure, using soft, manmade filling which gives a rounded shape and is machine washable. You could, however, use this type of cover on a foam pad for a more defined and boxy shape and a firmer seat. Such cushions are likely to get heavy wear, especially in a kitchen so choose sturdy, hardwearing fabric.

Perfect partners *Stripes and checks make perfect partners for these coordinating cushion covers. The outer cushion is tied on with lengths of ordinary tape or ribbon.*

PROJECT PLANNER

2 HOURS

Tools and Materials

Foam pad or cushion to fit your bench • Fabric for outer sleeve: the length of the cushion plus the depth plus 3cm (1¼in) x twice the width plus the depth plus 3cm (1¼in) • Fabric for inner sleeve: length of the cushion plus the depth plus 3cm (1¼in) x twice the width plus twice the depth plus 3cm (1¼in) • 1.2m (1⅜yd) of ribbon or tape for ties • Zip measuring three quarters of cushion length • Sewing machine and thread to match fabric

Inner sleeve

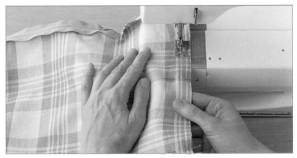

1 Fold the inner sleeve fabric in half lengthways, right sides together. Mark length of zip with pins. Machine stitch down to zip, taking a 1.5cm (⅝in) seam allowance, and backstitch to secure. Stitch below zip. Insert zip (see p.153).

2 Machine stitch side seams of the inner sleeve, taking a 1.5cm (⅝in) seam allowance.

3 Press side seams flat. Machine stitch across the corners at the point where the line of stitching is the same as the depth of the cushion to make the box shape (see p.137). Trim off excess fabric at the corner (see inset).

Outer sleeve

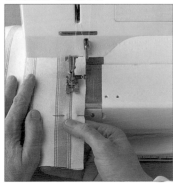

4 Fold fabric in half and pin and stitch side seams, taking a 1.5cm (⅝in) seam allowance. Box corners as in Step 3 (see p.137).

5 Press under a 1cm (⅜in) double hem to the wrong side all around the open edge and pin. Machine stitch close to the bottom edge and then machine stitch close to the top edge.

6 Cut four ties each measuring about 30cm (12in). Position one tie about one-third of the way from one end and the other one-third from the other end on the top of the cover. Pin the other two ties in the same position on the bottom of the cushion. To attach securely, turn under the raw end of the tie. Stitch round the end of the tie in a box shape and then stitch diagonally across (see p.146).

DRAGGED CUPBOARD DOORS

Gives a new look to old cupboards • Inexpensive • Classic Shaker style

GIVE THE DOORS of old kitchen units a sophisticated Shaker-style look with this simple dragging technique. You may be bored with your old units or have inherited some that are perfectly sound but simply not to your taste – this finish will cover a multitude of sins.

The doors are first covered with a coat of shellac-based primer. This can be used on any surface and provides a good surface to paint over. Take care when using this primer and always be sure to keep the room well ventilated while working. The primer ruins paintbrushes, too, so use an old one that can be thrown away afterwards. Once the primer is dry, two coats of white emulsion are applied. Finally the door is given a coat of creamy glaze and dragged to give a subtle yet textured finish. A coat of strong polyurethane varnish will protect the finished dragged doors from normal kitchen wear and tear.

New look
Battered old doors or ugly new ones can be transformed by this sleek, modern finish. Drag downwards on the centre panels and vertical stiles and across on the horizontal stiles.

PROJECT PLANNER

3 HOURS

Tools and Materials
Shellac-based primer • White vinyl matt emulsion • Cream vinyl matt emulsion • Scumble glaze • Old brush for primer • Paintbrushes • Dragging brush • Strong polyurethane varnish in satin or gloss • Sandpaper

2 Using an old brush, apply one coat of shellac-based primer. Leave to dry for about 30 minutes. This primer can be used over anything and gives a surface to work on without having to strip what is there. Make sure the area is well ventilated when using the primer.

1 Make sure the doors are clean and dry and free of any wax or grease. Sand down the doors to remove any uneven areas and make a smooth surface to ensure a fine finish.

3 Apply two coats of white vinyl matt emulsion to the doors. Leave each coat of paint until touch dry – about 30 minutes.

4 Mix a glaze from cream vinyl matt emulsion, scumble glaze and water (see p.165). Apply to the door a section at a time and drag while still wet. Take the dragging brush down from top to bottom in straight strokes. At the base, sweep the brush up slightly to avoid paint collecting. For horizontal stiles, drag the brush across.

5 Apply one coat of strong polyurethane satin varnish, or use gloss for a high shine. Brush the varnish in the same direction as the paint – vertically on the main part of the doors and across on the horizontal stiles.

CHECKED WALLS

Fresh, bright look • Quick and simple • Practical

THESE CHEERFUL checks give the look of wallpaper, but are much more practical in the hot, steamy atmosphere of a kitchen. Extremely simple to achieve, each pair of thick and thin stripes is produced with one stroke of a specially-cut foam roller. First the vertical stripes are applied and then the horizontal, working as smoothly as possible and keeping the roller as straight as you can. If you do need to stop in mid-stripe to put more paint on the roller, roll up the stripe slightly before stopping so that you don't get a tell-tale line.

Kitchen checks *Fresh and vibrant, these bright green checks make a perfect wall covering for a friendly family kitchen. For advice on working round doors and windows, see p.176.*

PROJECT PLANNER

3 HOURS

Tools and Materials
White vinyl matt emulsion • Vinyl matt emulsion in chosen colour • Mini-roller, usually 11cm (4¼in) wide • Paint tray • Masking tape • Scalpel or craft knife • Pencil • Ruler • Cutting board

1 *Prepare the wall (see p.169) and apply a base coat of white vinyl matt emulsion (see p.166). This will be the background to the checks. Leave the wall to dry for 30 minutes.*

2 *Take the mini-roller, mark a section 3cm (1¼in) from one end and cut out the foam (see p.174). This will give you one thick stripe and one thin stripe with each stroke of the roller.*

3 *Measure and mark the wall for the vertical stripes, using the width of the roller as the basis. Mark a dot for the right-hand edge of the first stripe. Allow for one set of stripes and a space of two roller widths and mark a dot for the right-hand edge of the next stripe. Mark each stripe at the top, middle and bottom of the wall.*

4 *Using the cut roller, apply the vertical stripes. Position roller carefully at the top of the wall with the right-hand edge against the mark each time and bring it down the wall, keeping as straight as you can. Press harder as you reach the bottom of the stripe to extract paint from the roller.*

5 *Take the ruler and make dots to mark the top edge of each horizontal stripe. This time leave a space of three roller widths between each set of stripes. Make several sets of marks across the wall to help you keep the roller straight.*

6 *Take the roller across the wall, positioning the top of the roller on the dot each time. Keep as straight as you can, but don't worry about any slight irregularities.*

CAFE CURTAIN

Makes a simple screen • Easy to remove and wash • Allows light into the room

A CAFE CURTAIN is a fresh and cheerful way to screen a dismal view or provide some privacy, while still allowing plenty of light into a room. Usually unlined and easy to remove and wash, café curtains are particularly suitable for kitchen windows but can be used in any room in the house.

The simplicity of this style suits curtains with minimal fullness. Whether they are gathered, box pleated as here, or even completely flat, you should allow a little ease in the width so that the curtain is not too taut on the rod.

The rod can be fixed at any height but usually looks best in line with the centre of the window frame. To attach the curtain to the rod, make a simple slot heading or eyelets through which the rod can be threaded or add sew-on rings to the top of the curtain. Perhaps the simplest method of all is to use café clips, available in many styles.

Semi-sheer
A café curtain made in a delicate fabric such as fine linen looks attractive and admits plenty of light. Instead of using clips, try attaching ribbons or ties to the pleats. These are simply looped round the rod and tied in place.

PROJECT PLANNER

Tools and Materials

Fabric: length of area of window to be covered plus 7.5cm (3in) hem allowance x width of window, plus extra width for pleats (see p.154), plus 25cm (10in) for fullness and for side hem and seam allowances • Rod to fit window • Café clips, allowing one for every pleat and one for each end • Sewing machine and thread to match fabric

1 *If necessary, join widths with a french seam (see p.134). Fold, press and pin a 2.5cm (1in) double hem down both sides of the curtain and along the bottom edge, making mitred corners (see p.137) as shown. Machine stitch the hems.*

2 *Fold, press and pin a 12mm (½in) double hem at the top of the curtain. The corners of the top hem do not need to be mitred. Machine stitch.*

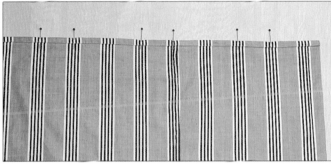

3 *Mark the positions of the pleats with pins. The width of each pleat shown here is 7.5cm (3in) and the pleats are 12.5cm (6in) apart. (See p.154 for more information on measuring and marking pleats.)*

4 *To make a pleat, fold right sides of the fabric together, so that the pins marking each side of the pleat meet as shown. Place another pin 7.5cm (3in) down from the top of the curtain to hold the pleat in place and to mark the depth of stitching. Fold all the pleats in the same way.*

5 *Machine stitch each pleat along the line of the marker pins, working from the top of the curtain down to the pin marking the base of the pleat.*

6 *Press the pleats flat as shown. Attach a clip to each pleat and one to each top corner of the curtain. Thread the clip rings onto the rod.*

STENCILLED TILES

New look for old tiles • Inexpensive and easy to do • Create your own design

CERAMIC TILES are expensive to replace simply because you no longer like their colour and this project is an ideal way of disguising them. First, the tiles are given a coat of primer which prepares the surface for painting. Then the tiles are painted with vinyl matt emulsion in your chosen colour. Now you can let your imagination run riot with stencils. Here, the radish and carrot echo the kitchen theme but there are a wealth of attractive designs to choose from. Alternatively, try making stencils to your own design (see p.172 and p.184).

For the best results, be sure to place the stencils very carefully, so that they are in the same position on the tile each time. Work out a pattern of blank and stencilled tiles rather than stencil every one and keep to a limited palette of colours so the effect is not too 'busy'. Varnish the finished wall to protect it from moisture and wear and tear.

Kitchen partners *A carrot and radish make ideal stencil partners for this kitchen tiling. The original tiles have been covered in simple white emulsion to make a perfect backdrop for the stencil colours.*

PROJECT PLANNER

4 HOURS

Tools and Materials

Tile primer • White vinyl matt emulsion • Stencil paint or artist's acrylic paint in red, orange, raw umber, burnt umber, dark and light green, and white • Gloss polyurethane varnish • Ready-cut stencils or stencils made to your own design (see p.172 and p.184) • Stencil brushes • Mini-roller • Low-tack masking tape • Brush for varnish

1 *Following the manufacturer's instructions, apply a coat of tile primer to tiles. Always use primer in a well-ventilated room. When the primer is dry, apply a coat of white vinyl matt emulsion to the tiles.*

2 *Take your stencils and decide on your design. Here two stencils are used and every other tile is stencilled. If possible, cut the stencil to fit the tile. Otherwise mark the midpoint of each tile and make sure the same part of the stencil is at the midpoint each time. Attach the stencils to the tiles with masking tape.*

3 *Using the stencil brush, stipple on the paint. For the carrot stencil used here, stipple light green onto the leaves. Add some dark green but leave the tips light. Stipple the carrot with orange and highlight the top edge with a little white and the bottom edge with a tiny touch of raw umber.*

4 *Stipple the leaves of the radish in light green and add a little dark green to the undersides. Stipple the radish in red and add a little burnt umber to the bottom edge. Highlight the radish root with a touch of white. Remove the stencils and repeat the motifs as necessary.*

5 *When all the stencils are complete, allow them to dry thoroughly before varnishing. Use a roller to avoid brush marks and apply one coat of gloss polyurethane varnish.*

Garden Rooms

VERDIGRIS CHAIR

Revives old furniture • Provides weather-proofing • Adds character

AN OLD METAL garden chair can be given a new lease of life with this faux verdigris technique and even coordinated with other junk-shop finds. First, the chair must be carefully sanded to remove any old paint and given a coat of rust-proofing paint. The pinkness of this is then disguised with a watery coat of raw umber. The verdigris effect is simulated by dabbing the chair first with pale turquoise emulsion and then with dark green. The dark green should be applied in irregular patches, allowing some turquoise to show through.

Patina of time *Real verdigris is the bluish-green sheen which forms on metal as it is corroded by the elements over time. Painted verdigris mimics this look while weather-proofing the chair.*

PROJECT PLANNER

3 HOURS

Tools and Materials

Rust-proofing paint • Raw umber artist's acrylic • Pale turquoise vinyl matt emulsion • Green vinyl matt emulsion • Matt polyurethane varnish • Paintbrushes • Brush for varnishing • Sandpaper • Pieces of sponge or old foam roller

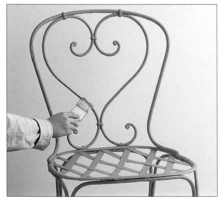

1 *Sand the chair well to remove any flakes or other debris. Apply a coat of rust-proofing paint to all surfaces and allow to dry for about 30 minutes.*

2 *Mix some raw umber artist's acrylic with water to a watery consistency. Paint the chair with this mixture, not to cover it but to disguise the pinkness of the rust-proofing paint.*

3 *Take some pieces of sponge or tear an old foam roller into several bits. Using a piece of sponge or foam, dab pale turquoise vinyl matt emulsion all over the chair. Don't worry if some small areas of umber still show. Allow to dry.*

4 *Take a new piece of sponge and dab dark green vinyl matt emulsion onto the chair in irregular patches so that some of the paler colour still shows through. Use a small brush if necessary to reach any awkward areas. Leave to dry.*

5 *Using a soft brush, apply one coat of matt polyurethane varnish to the chair.*

STENCILLED FLOOR RUG

Unusual floor treatment • Practical yet effective • Adaptable to space available

A PAINTED AND stencilled floor rug is a surprisingly practical way of adding colour and decoration to a garden room. Once the rug is protected with varnish, it is easy to clean and wears well. It also has the advantage of being cheap to do and relatively simple to change should you tire of the design. And unlike a fabric rug, there is nothing to trip over as you walk through the room laden with plant pots.

Before you start, give careful thought to the shape of the room and the size of the floor rug. Measure the floor carefully and plan the design to scale. It can be a simple coloured shape with stencil frieze as here, or something much more complex, perhaps taking inspiration from oriental rugs. Once the design is planned, mark the area on the floor and mask off the edges. Paint in the background colour and then add the stencil frieze, positioning them with great care to keep the design neat and symmetrical. When the rug is complete, it is essential to add two coats of good quality floor varnish to protect it from dirt and constant footsteps.

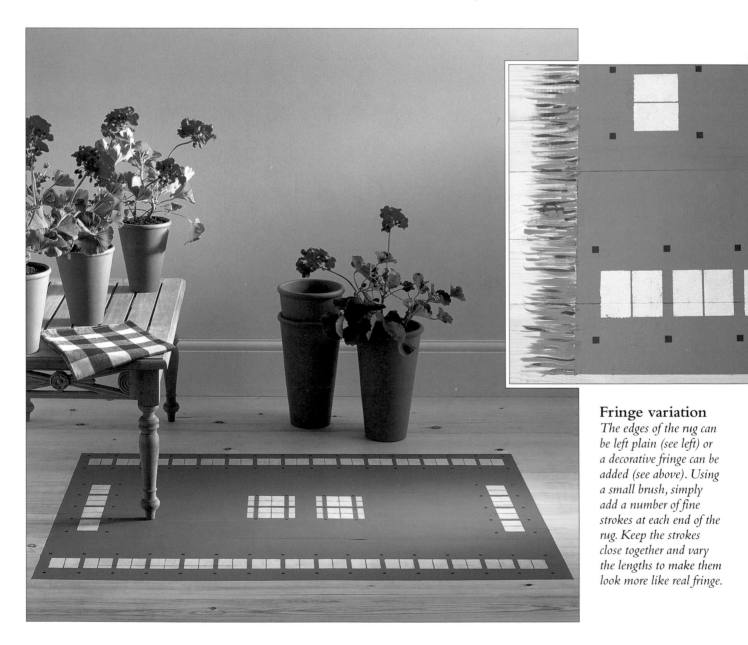

Fringe variation
The edges of the rug can be left plain (see left) or a decorative fringe can be added (see above). Using a small brush, simply add a number of fine strokes at each end of the rug. Keep the strokes close together and vary the lengths to make them look more like real fringe.

PROJECT PLANNER

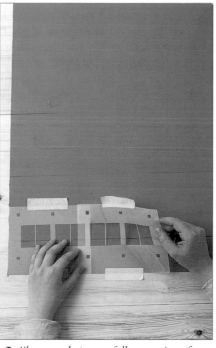

Tools and Materials
Green vinyl matt emulsion • Artist's acrylic in three colours • Stencils (geometric designs are most suitable) • Stencil brushes • Paintbrush • Masking tape • Pencil • Ruler • Polyurethane floor varnish

2½ HOURS

1 Decide on the extent of your rug and mark it out on the floor, using a pencil and ruler. The example here measures 114 x 76cm (45 x 30in).

2 Place masking tape all round the outside edges of the marked area. Paint the area with green vinyl matt emulsion and leave to dry. Remove the masking tape.

3 Plan your design carefully on a piece of paper. Place the first stencils on the painted area. Make sure you overlap them correctly.

4 Using a stencilling brush, stipple in artist's acrylic paint on the stencils, using the colours in a regular design. Remove the stencils and reposition. Continue to make a frieze down both sides of the rug and at each end.

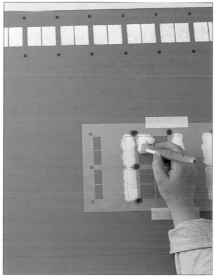

5 Position stencils in the middle and stipple in colours. Repeat as required, again making sure you overlap the stencils correctly.

6 Allow the stencilling to dry. Apply two coats of good-quality polyurethane floor varnish over the whole rug to protect it.

DISTRESSED DOOR
Adds a naturally aged look • Disguises a scruffy door • Quick and easy

THIS TECHNIQUE recreates the look of paintwork that has darkened and become worn and cracked over time. It can be used to age a new door or disguise battered old wood and gives a pleasantly countrified and informal feel, particularly well suited to a garden room. The door is painted with a coat of dark green emulsion and furniture wax is then applied to areas that would receive the

hardest wear and tear. A coat of cream paint is applied over the green and the waxed areas rubbed with wire wool to give a naturally worn look.

A country look *Distressed paintwork makes this old farmhouse door an ideal partner for the rustic brick walls and casual atmosphere of this pleasant garden room.*

PROJECT PLANNER

2½ HOURS

Tools and Materials
Dark green vinyl matt emulsion • Cream vinyl matt emulsion • Wire wool • Furniture wax • Paintbrushes • Rubber gloves • Sandpaper • Mutton cloth

1 *Sand the door carefully to remove any rough areas and create a smooth surface.*

2 *Apply a coat of dark green vinyl matt emulsion to the door. The coverage can be quite rough. Allow to dry for 30 minutes.*

3 *Take some rag or mutton cloth and apply furniture wax to the areas you want to look distressed. Concentrate on those that are likely to be particularly worn, such as the area around the latch and the central stile.*

4 *Apply a coat of cream vinyl matt emulsion to the door and leave to dry for 30 minutes. Again, the finish does not have to be perfect.*

5 *Always wear rubber gloves when working with wire wool. Take a big pad of wire wool and rub over the areas where you applied wax – these will appear slightly whiter than the rest of the door. Rub them vigorously until the green shows through. Keep rubbing until the door has a naturally aged look.*

6 HOURS

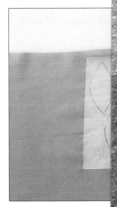

3 *Take one pillowca...*
pillowcase, starting...
sure that all the leaves...
the arrangement, iron...
manufacturer's instruc...

BEDROOMS

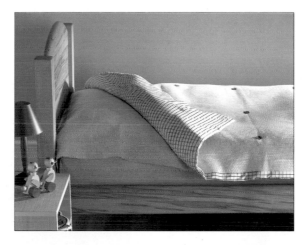

LINED BASKETS

Quick to make • Inexpensive storage method • Versatile and attractive

Makes pl

ESPITE T
market,
coordin
designs that won
One solution
cotton bedlinen
design in the c
difficult if you u

OR A PRACTICAL and pretty storage solution for clothes and linen in the bedroom, use wicker baskets of varying sizes and stack them on deep shelves. Make simple fabric linings to tie inside the baskets to protect your delicate items of clothing from catching and snagging on the wickerwork.

Almost any fabric can be used. Coordinate the basket linings with other soft furnishings in the bedroom, for instance, or use a feminine floral chintz with narrow satin ribbons for ties. For a country look, choose bright gingham or ticking stripes, or go for quiet simplicity with starched white linen and natural linen tape like the ones shown here. Make sure that the fabric you choose is washable. If there is any risk of shrinkage, wash the fabric before you start to make the linings.

The basket linings are simple to make. The fabric is cut out, following the diagram opposite and the dimensions of the basket, and stitched together at the corners. The ties are then attached at each corner and the top of the lining is turned over and machined.

Decorative linings
Slender ties are threaded through gaps in the wickerwork and fastened in a bow to hold the lining in place.

PROJECT PLANNER

Tools and Materials

Fabric for one: the length of basket plus twice the depth plus 4cm (1½in) seam allowances x the width of basket plus twice the depth plus 4cm (1½in) seam allowances • 2.5m (2½yd) linen tape or ribbon for ties • Sewing machine and thread to match fabric

1¼ HOURS

Plan for liner fabric

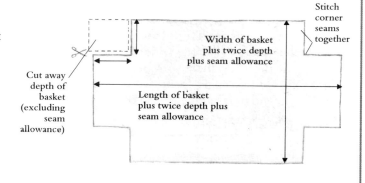

Stitch corner seams together

Width of basket plus twice depth plus seam allowance

Cut away depth of basket (excluding seam allowance)

Length of basket plus twice depth plus seam allowance

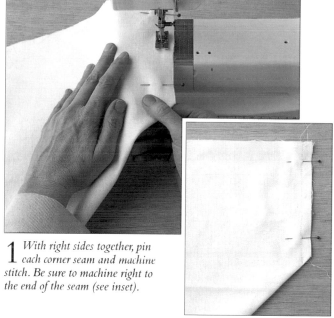

1 *With right sides together, pin each corner seam and machine stitch. Be sure to machine right to the end of the seam (see inset).*

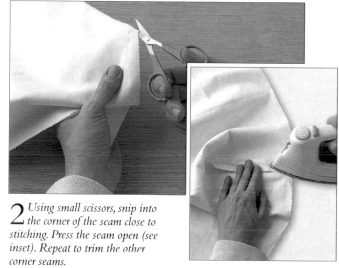

2 *Using small scissors, snip into the corner of the seam close to stitching. Press the seam open (see inset). Repeat to trim the other corner seams.*

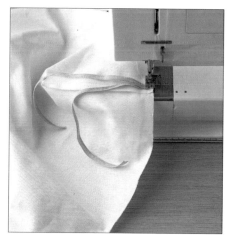

3 *Cut four ties each about 60cm (24in) long. Fold one tie in half and pin with the folded edge at the top of a corner seam. Machine stitch across the top of the tie, keeping very close to the top of the fabric. Repeat to attach the other ties.*

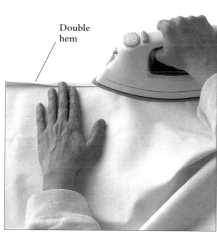

Double hem

4 *Fold over a 1cm (⅜in) double hem at the top edge of the basket lining. Press and pin.*

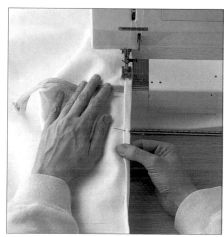

5 *Machine stitch all round the hem, keeping close to the folded edge, and keeping the ends of the ties out of the way.*

SIMPLE QUILT

Light but cosy • Made by hand • An attractive extra layer

THIS COSY QUILT makes a useful extra layer or a lightweight cover for the summer months. It is made from one piece of fabric bonded to polyester wadding, with another contrasting piece of fabric laid underneath and folded up and over the raw edges. The layers are quilted together with small discs of wool or felt, stitched in place with french knots. To estimate the size, measure the made-up bed and allow for a generous cover.

Use fabric that feels soft to the touch, particularly for the underneath layer. As always, when you are using several different fabrics together, check that they are pre-shrunk and colourfast. Wash them all beforehand if necessary.

Textural interest *The quilt here is made from fabrics with contrasting textures rather than pattern to create interest – a strong cotton waffle teamed with a smooth checked lawn.*

PROJECT PLANNER

3 HOURS

Tools and Materials

Fabric for top panel: to fit bed • Fabric for bottom panel: finished size of quilt plus 4cm (1½in) all round • 113g (4oz) wadding cut to finished size of quilt plus 2.5cm (1in) all round • Embellishments: 25cm (10in) of contrast fabric • Embroidery silk • Art and craft spray adhesive • Thread to match fabric

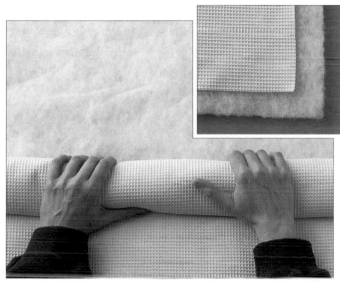

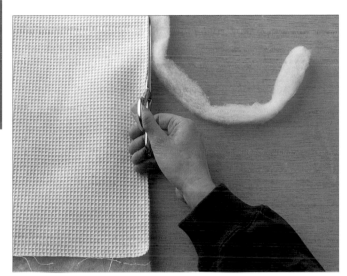

1 *Roll up the main panel fabric. Lay the wadding down and place the fabric over it, wrong side down to check size. The wadding will extend beyond the edge of the fabric (see inset) but will be trimmed to fit. Roll the fabric back again and spray the wadding with adhesive. Working quickly but carefully, unroll the wadding over the fabric.*

2 *Trim off the excess wadding to fit the fabric exactly. Note that it is better to have too much wadding and then trim to fit than to try to calculate the exact amount.*

3 *Take the bottom panel and place it wrong side up. Press over the edges 1cm (⅜in) and then 3cm (1¼in) all round. At the corners, allow the short edges to overlap the long edges.*

4 *With the wadding face down, place the top panel over the bottom panel, tucking the edges under the folded edges of the bottom panel. Neatly slipstitch (see p.138) the folded edges of the bottom panel to the top fabric.*

5 *Measure your quilt and decide how many embellishments you want to add. Measure and mark their positions. Make the embellishments (see p 157) and stitch each one in place through all layers of fabric with a french knot (see p 139) in embroidery silk.*

CLOUD DOOR

Easy and fun • Perfect for a child's room • Adds a decorative feature

THIS IS A WONDERFUL finish for a door in a child's bedroom and should help to induce sweet dreams. It creates a magical effect that you don't need to be an expert artist to achieve – anyone can paint clouds.

When you apply the blue glaze to the door, try to keep the colour stronger at the top, gradually decreasing toward the bottom. Don't apply the clouds too heavily – they should be delicate and slightly translucent like the real things. Vary the shapes of the clouds and make sure that you have some coming in from each side of the door.

Blue skies *Puffy white clouds on a bright blue sky make an ordinary bedroom door into a cheerful feature and shouldn't tax anyone's artistic skills.*

PROJECT PLANNER

3½ HOURS

Tools and Materials
White satin emulsion • Blue artist's acrylic • White artist's acrylic • Scumble glaze • Gloss polyurethane varnish • Paintbrushes • Softening brush

1 *If the door is already painted, sand it down. Apply a coat of white satin emulsion and allow to dry for at least 30 minutes.*

2 *Mix a glaze with blue artist's acrylic, scumble glaze and water (see p.165). Apply the glaze in sections, starting at the top of the door and using horizontal strokes to work back and forth across the door. Use plenty of paint so that the section at the top of the door appears to be the darkest.*

3 *While the first section of glaze is still damp, go over it with a softening brush to disguise the brush marks. Once the first section is softened, continue painting and softening the door in sections. Use slightly less paint as you work down the door so it becomes lighter towards the bottom.*

4 *Using a small amount of white artist's acrylic paint, start making the clouds with swirling, rounded strokes. Indicate the main shape of the cloud first and then add more white, but don't allow them to get too heavy – they should retain some translucency.*

5 *With a little more white paint on the brush than before, add some white highlights to the edges of the clouds. Take care not to overdo it. Leave to dry for an hour.*

6 *Apply a coat of gloss polyurethane varnish to the finished door and leave to dry completely.*

108

BATHROOMS

BATHROOM ORGANISER

A stylish way of storing clutter • Adaptable pocket sizes •Waterproof finish

HERE IS A HANDY hanging organiser in which to store the many bits and pieces which tend to clutter a bathroom. You can make the organiser to the exact size shown here or adapt it to fit your own requirements, with pockets designed to accommodate particular items. Choose two stylish but sturdy coordinating fabrics. Spray both with fabric protector to give the cloth a water-resistant finish before you start to make up the organiser or choose PVC-coated fabrics. Hang the finished organiser behind a door or from hooks on the wall. Alternatively, if you prefer to hang the organiser from a towel rail, make long ties instead of loops at the top.

Pocket sizes
Think about the items you wish to keep in your organiser and calculate the pocket sizes to suit. You can vary the depth of the pockets and divide them up vertically to make individual pockets.

PROJECT PLANNER

2 HOURS

Tools and Materials

Fabric for main panels: one top panel 30 x 116.5cm (12 x 46in) and one base panel 40 x 121.5cm (16 x 50in) • Fabric for pockets: two pockets 30 x 30cm (12 x 12in) deep and three pockets 30 x 20cm (12 x 8in) deep • Fabric for two bias-cut ties with finished size of 12mm x 25cm (½ x 10in) (see p.148) • Fabric protector spray • Sewing machine and thread to match fabric

1 *Before starting to sew, spray both sides of all pieces of fabric with fabric protector to make them water resistant. Follow the manufacturer's instructions when spraying.*

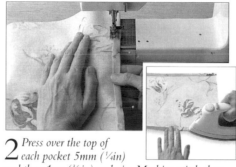

2 *Press over the top of each pocket 5mm (¼in) and then 1cm (⅜in) and pin. Machine stitch close to the folded edge. Press over the bottom edge of all except the bottom pocket 1.5cm (⅝in) (see inset).*

3 *Take the top panel and place right side up. Starting at the bottom, place the pockets right side up on the panel, butting them up to one another, and leaving about 10cm (4in) free at the top. Pin in place.*

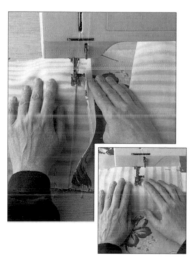

4 *Machine stitch across the base of each pocket, working close to the folded edge each time. When you reach the bottom pocket, stitch it with the bottom edge flat, not folded. Divide one pocket into two and another into three by machine stitching from top to bottom (see inset). Backstitch at the start and finish to secure the stitching.*

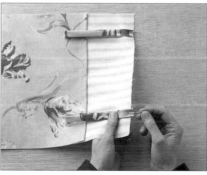

5 *Make two bias cut ties (see p.148), each 12mm (½in) wide by 25cm (10in) long. Fold each tie in half and position at the top of the top panel, raw edges aligned. Machine stitch across the ties to hold them in place.*

6 *Take the base panel. Press over 2.5cm (1in) double hems at the sides and base, mitring corners (see p.137).*

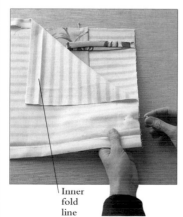

Inner fold line

7 *With right sides together, place the base panel over the top panel, aligning centres. Open out the folds on the base panel and pin the panels together across the top. Machine stitch 1.5cm (⅝in) from the top, starting from the inner fold line of the base panel and stitching across to the other inner fold line.*

8 *Fold the base panel over to the back. Tuck the top panel under the folded edges of the base panel and pin the panels together along sides and base.*

9 *Machine stitch all round. Start at the top corner and keeping close to the inner folded edge, stitch down one side, around the corner and across the base and then up the other side. Hand sew the diagonal corners using even slipstitch (see p.138).*

SHOWER CURTAIN

Simple but effective • Make to fit your shower • Individual design

CREATE YOUR OWN shower curtain from stark white PVC and chrome eyelets, but add a feminine touch with a pretty lace-effect edging down each side of the curtain. If you have white tiles, think of using a coloured material or the lace effect will be lost. PVC fabric is only available in one width, but if you need to screen off the length of a bath, make two curtains that meet in the middle.

Experiment with the template on some spare fabric before you start so you are sure to get it right on the real thing. Try varying the pattern with scallops but keep it simple.

A lacy look *The lace effect, made using pinking shears and a leather hole punch, is very effective, particularly when set against coloured tiles or paint effects around your bath or shower.*

PROJECT PLANNER

2½ HOURS

Tools and Materials

Main fabric (PVC or similar waterproof material): measure the distance from the shower rail to the floor and add 5cm (2in) for top hem x width of fabric or 1¼ times shower rail • Card for template • Water-based felt pen • Pinking shears • Leather punch • Eyelet kit • Hammer

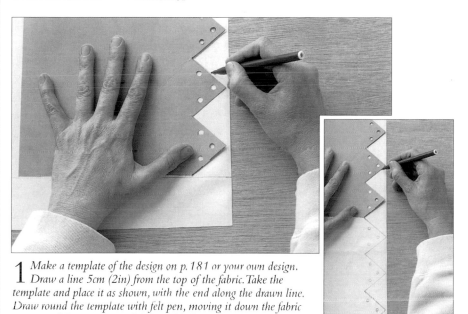

1 *Make a template of the design on p.181 or your own design. Draw a line 5cm (2in) from the top of the fabric. Take the template and place it as shown, with the end along the drawn line. Draw round the template with felt pen, moving it down the fabric as required (see inset). Mark holes with dots.*

2 *Using a pair of pinking shears, trim off the end above the drawn line as shown. Then cut around the line of the template.*

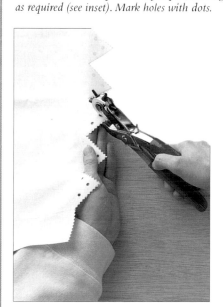

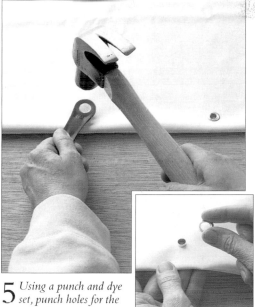

3 *Take a leather punch and carefully punch out all the marked holes. Repeat Steps 1 to 3 down the other side of the curtain.*

4 *Turn the fabric over at the marked fold line. Mark the position of the first eyelet about 2.5cm (1in) in from the end. Mark the positions of the remaining eyelets at approximately 15cm (6in) intervals across the top of the curtain.*

5 *Using a punch and dye set, punch holes for the eyelets at the marked positions, following the instructions with your kit. Insert the base of the eyelet through the hole from the right side of the curtain. Place the backing ring over the top (see inset) and hammer on. Clean off any marks.*

FROSTED GLASS PANEL

Decorative • Simple to do • Creates a stylish screen

T HE DELICATE, translucent look of real frosted or etched glass can be easily achieved with the help of frosting spray and is a perfect way to add decorative interest to a plain, glass-panelled door. Cut-out shapes are placed on the glass before spraying the frosting. When these are removed, the unfrosted areas of glass beneath are revealed, creating an attractive pattern. If the shapes are kept reasonably small, the frosting also provides some privacy. Always wear a face mask and keep windows open when using any kind of spray product.

A subtle screen *Sea creatures and fronds of seaweed strike a jaunty marine note on this bathroom door. The snowy frosting creates a subtle screen and is a simple way to provide some privacy.*

PROJECT PLANNER

2 HOURS

Tools and Materials
Frosting spray • Face mask • Cut-out shapes or reverse stencils • Mounting spray glue • Newspaper • Masking tape • Glass cleaner

1 *Use the shapes on p. 185 or designs of your choice to make the masking shapes. Take some sheets of newspaper and, using masking tape, fix them all round the pane of glass to protect the woodwork and walls. Be careful to tape the paper right at the edge of the pane so that no glass is covered by the newspaper. Make sure the glass is clean and dry.*

2 *Decide how you want to place your shapes. Spray the back of a shape with mounting spray and place carefully on the glass. Repeat with all the shapes to make the desired design (see inset).*

3 *Apply the frosting spray all over the glass panel, making sure the coverage is as even as possible. Wear a mask when using the spray and make sure the room is well ventilated. Allow the frosting spray to dry for about 15 minutes.*

4 *Carefully peel off the shapes to reveal the unfrosted areas beneath. Leave for about half an hour and then wipe off any remaining glue with glass cleaner.*

SEWING TECHNIQUES

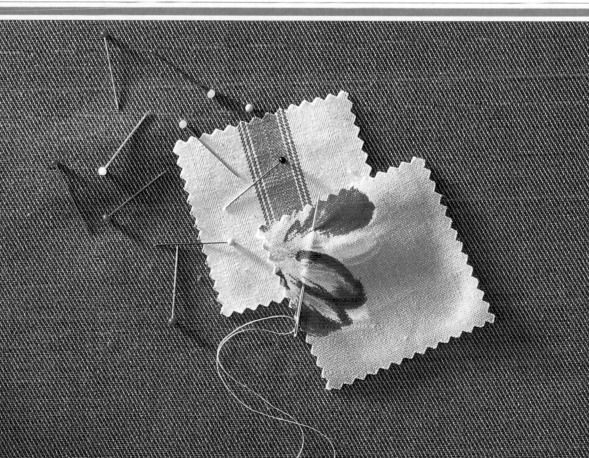

EQUIPMENT

The soft furnishing projects in this book do not require a lot of sophisticated equipment. For most, a sewing machine is essential and it is useful, but not vital, to have a model that can do zigzag stitching and buttonholes. Always have an iron close at hand – seam and hem allowances need to be pressed in place. Other basic items include good sharp scissors for cutting fabric, plus smaller scissors for other tasks. A fabric tape measure is useful for measuring small areas such as hems, but you may also like to have a wooden rule for measuring larger extents on your work surface.

Sewing

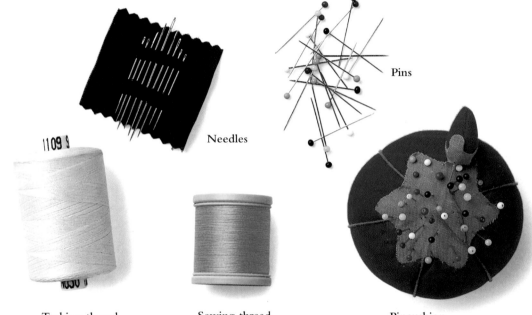

Pins, needles and thread

Pins, needles and thread are essential items for any sewing box. Plain pins are fine, but pins with coloured plastic heads are easier to find and remove from large swathes of fabric. A pincushion is a useful way of ensuring that pins stay in the right place. Sewing thread is used for general hand and machine sewing. It can also be used for temporary tacking, but soft tacking thread is easier to remove.

Sewing machine

If possible, your sewing machine should have a zigzag facility, a piping foot and a buttonhole foot for the projects in this book.

Needles

Pins

Pincushion

Tacking thread

Sewing thread

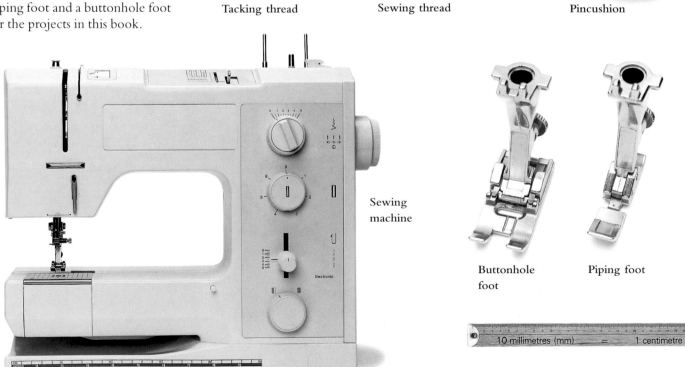

Sewing machine

Buttonhole foot

Piping foot

10 millimetres (mm)   =   1 centimetre (cm)

Measuring, Cutting and Pressing

Cutting tools

A pair of good-quality dressmaker's scissors will make all the difference to your sewing projects, enabling you to cut fabric efficiently. Never use your fabric scissors on paper – it will dull the blades. Pinking shears are useful for finishing the raw edges of seams (see p.133) and you will also need smaller scissors for tasks such as clipping seams. A stitch ripper is better than scissors for removing stitching from fabric.

Markers and measures

Tailor's chalk is ideal for marking fabric because it dusts off easily. You may also need pencils and markers for making templates. A tape measure is essential – never guess the measurements of a project.

Iron

A steam iron and ironing board should always be on hand for pressing fabrics.

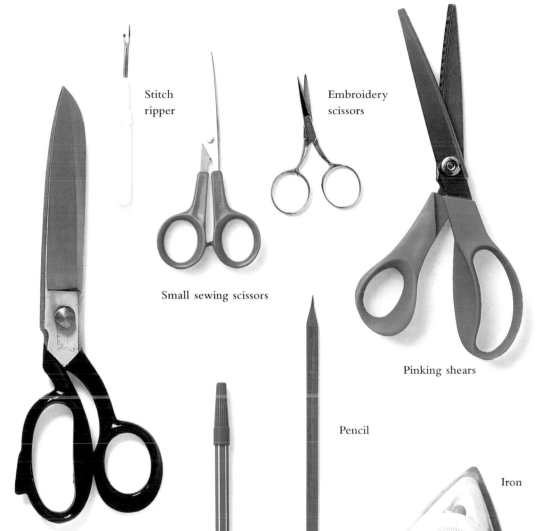

Stitch ripper

Embroidery scissors

Small sewing scissors

Pinking shears

Pencil

Dressmaker's scissors

Iron

Water-soluble marker

Tailor's chalk

Tape measure

| 100 centimetres (cm) | = | 1 metre (m) | 1000 metres (m) | = | 1 kilometre (km) |

Wooden rule

MEASURING AND ESTIMATING

Always measure and estimate fabric requirements accurately before starting projects. For curtains and blinds, take two basic measurements – the 'finished width' and the 'finished length'. To work out the 'working width'(the width to cut), add an allowance for fullness to the finished width. To work out the 'working length'(the length to cut), add an allowance for hems and headings to the finished length. If using a patterned fabric, add an allowance for matching the pattern (see page opposite). For curtains, it is best to install the track or pole from which they will hang before you start. As a rule, tracks and poles are usually fitted 10–15cm (4–6in) above the window frame and extend 15–20cm (6-8in) each side, as space permits, to allow room for the curtains to hang when drawn back.

Measuring a Window for Curtains

Once your track or pole is up, measure the width first, then the length. Jot your measurements down as soon as you have taken them to avoid getting them wrong. It is essential to use an extendible metal tape measure as a fabric measure will give inaccurate measurements.

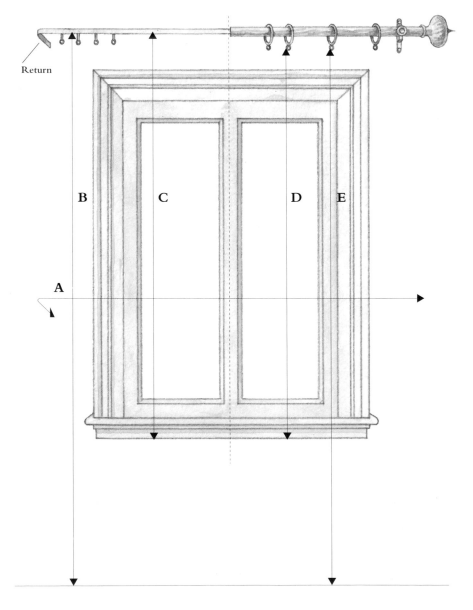

Return

B   C   D   E

A

Finished width Measure the entire span of the track or pole (**A**). If the track projects from the wall, include the return (the distance it projects from the wall) at both ends in your measurement. If the track has an overlap arm that meets in the centre, add the amount of overlap to the width.

Finished length Take the top of the track (**B** and **C**), or the bottom of the curtain rings on a pole (**D** and **E**) as the starting point for your finished length measurement. (For slot-, tie- or tab-headed curtains measure from the pole top). Measure down to the sill (**C** and **D**) or floor (**B** and **E**). Subtract 1cm (½in) if you want curtains to clear the floor, or add 2.5cm (1in) if you want them on the floor.

To estimate the amount of fabric Decide how much fullness you want for your curtains. 1½ times the width for flat or tab headed curtains, 2 or 2½ times the width for gathered or pleated headings. Multiply the finished width measurement by the amount of fullness you want to reach your working width. Divide the working width by the width of your fabric and round the answer up to the next whole number to get the number of widths or 'drops' you will need. For a pair of curtains, divide this by 2 for the number of widths in each curtain. Add up to 30cm (12in) for hem and heading allowance to the finished length measurement to get your working length. If there is a pattern repeat allow extra for that (see page opposite).

Multiply the working length measurement by the number of drops required to reach your overall fabric requirement.

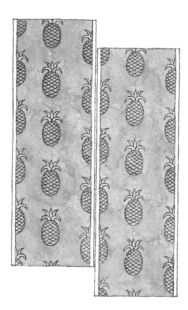

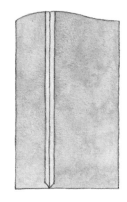
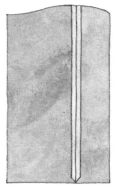

Estimating extra fabric for pattern repeat

Once you have the working length, measure the length of a complete pattern on your fabric. Divide the working length by the pattern length. Round this up to the next whole number and multiply by the pattern length. This will give you the amount of fabric you need to cut to match the pattern across widths.

Joining widths and half widths

If a pair of curtains requires three widths, cut one width in half and make each curtain of one and a half widths. Place the half width at the outside of the curtain and the full width in the centre.

Measuring a Window for a Blind

A blind is usually fitted to a wooden lath, usually 5 x 2.5cm (2 x 1in) softwood cut to the finished width of the blind. Before you start, decide where the lath is to be fixed – to the wall above the window, to the top of the window frame (or architrave), or, if the window is recessed, to the inside of the recess.

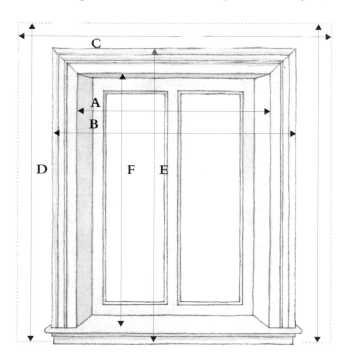

Finished width Measure the width of the area you wish the blind to cover – either the width of the recess (**A**), the width of the architrave (**B**) or wider if you want the blind to extend to either side of the window frame (**C**). For a recessed window, to ensure that the blind moves freely up and down, deduct 2cm (¾in) from the width of the recess.

Finished length This is usually dictated by where the blind is mounted in the window area. If the blind is hanging from the wall above the window, it should drop to just below the sill (**D**); if it is attached to the frame, it should drop to the sill, or just below it (**E**); and if it is mounted inside the recess, it can only drop to the sill (**F**). Some blinds need extra length for fullness when they are down (see Blind with Ties p.14).

Working measurements For the working width of a blind, add two side hem allowances to the finished width measurement. Allow 5cm (2in) for each or see individual project. For the working length, add a hem and a heading allowance to the finished length measurement. Allow 5cm (2in) for each or see individual project. It is best to allow at least 5cm (2in) extra at the top of the blind. This allows room for error and any excess can be trimmed off before finishing the heading.

Estimating fabric Divide the working width by the width of your fabric. If the answer is less than one, you will only need one width of fabric and the total length of fabric required is the working length. If the answer is more than one you will have to join widths of fabric to get the full working width of the blind. The extra width is usually divided in two and joined to either side of the first width, so that there is a central panel and two joining seams. To work out the amount of fabric you need, multiply the number of widths required by the working length (plus any extra required to match a pattern, see above).

Measuring a Cushion Pad

When making several cushion covers, it is worth making a paper template
of the cushion pad first. Do not add seam allowances so the covers will fit snugly, making
the finished cushions look pleasingly plump.

For a conventional cover with a top and bottom
piece, simply measure the width and length of
the pad. For an envelope cushion, measure the
width but allow twice the length plus about
20cm (8in) for the envelope flap.

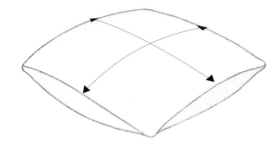

Measuring a Bolster

A standard bolster cushion is 46cm (18in) long, with a diameter of 18cm (7in).
The simplest method of covering a bolster is to make a long cover that ties at each end
like a Christmas cracker and extends into a frill.

Measure the circumference and length of the
bolster and across each end for the diameter. For
a cover without a separate end piece, measure
from the centre of one end, down the length to
the centre of the other end. Add to this
measurement enough extra length to gather the
fabric together and form a cracker end. Add
seam allowances of 1.5cm (⅝in) all round.

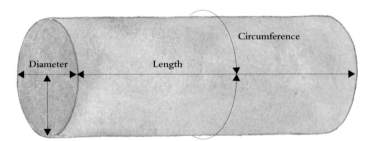

Measuring a Box Cushion

A conventional box cushion has a top and bottom piece, and a 'stand' (or depth)
that runs all round the sides of the cushion. A simpler method of covering a box cushion is to make
a flat cover and mitre the corners to make a box shape.

In this simple method of covering a box
cushion, the flat cover has to include the 'stand'
or depth measurement as well as the length and
width. Measure the length of the cushion and
add one depth measurement. Then measure the
width of the cushion, double that and add
twice the depth of the pad. Finally add seam
allowances of 1.5cm (⅝in) all round.

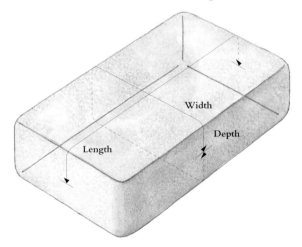

Measuring a Chair

A squab cushion should fit a chair seat neatly, so start by
making a paper template of the seat area. Place the paper on the chair seat
and trace around the shape with a pencil.

Measure the length and width of the chair.
Make the template on the generous side so that
the edges of the paper extend slightly beyond
the edges of the chair. Once the cushion pad is
covered with stockinette and the tightly fitting
cover, it will be slightly smaller than the
original template and a cushion that is too
small for the seat looks uncomfortable and
mean. Mark where the chair struts extend from
the seat so that you will know where to attach
ties to the cover.

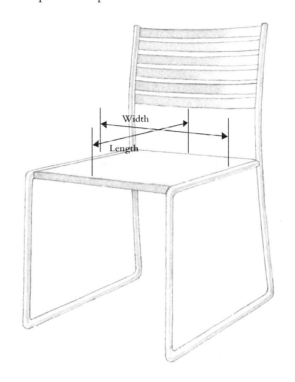

Measuring a Table

For a rectangular tablecloth, first decide on how much overhang you want.
Sit at a chair and measure from the top of the table to just above your lap. Alternatively, you may
want to make a longer cloth that reaches to the floor.

Measure the length and
width of the tabletop. Add
twice your desired overhang
measurement to both the
length and width of the
tabletop and then add seam
allowances all round to
obtain the overall dimen-
sions of the cloth. If adding
a border to the tablecloth,
subtract the depth of the
border from the overall
width and length measure-
ment. For the border, cut
fabric twice the finished
depth plus seam allowances.

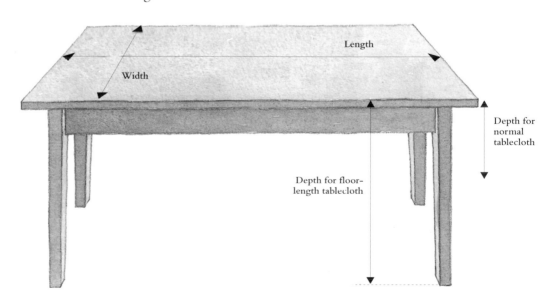

CUTTING AND STITCHING

Before you start any soft furnishing project, make sure that you have everything you need in terms of equipment and that your sewing machine is in good working order. Take exact measurements – whether of windows, cushion pads or furniture – with great care and always double check them before starting to cut fabric.

When cutting, use really sharp scissors. A pair of good quality dressmaker's scissors will last for years and make your task much easier. None of the projects in this book is difficult, but a little attention to detail before you start will make all the difference and help you achieve a satisfying and professional-looking result.

Cutting on the Grain

Fabric is usually cut directly down or across the material
on the horizontal or vertical grain. It is particularly important that curtains and blinds
are cut absolutely square or they will not hang correctly.

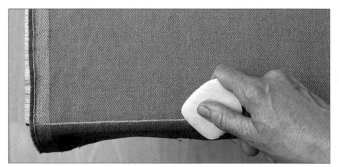

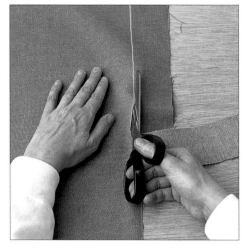

1 *To make sure that you have a straight edge at right angles to the selvedge, place the fabric flat on a table, with the selvedge aligned along one side. Allow the fabric to hang slightly over the edge of the table. Draw a line with tailor's chalk along the table edge to mark the straight grain as shown.*

2 *Place the fabric on the table and cut along the chalked line, keeping as straight as possible. Work from this straight edge when measuring and cutting the fabric. Use sharp scissors, preferably with long blades.*

Cutting on the Bias

Fabric cut on the bias moulds around curves and corners
more easily, so use bias-cut fabric for ties that are to be tied into bows
and for piping to fit round shapes.

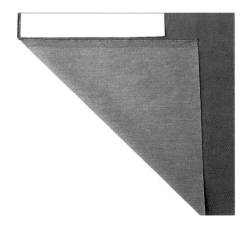

1 *Fold in a corner of a width of fabric at a right angle. Check that the angle is correct by aligning the fabric with a piece of paper as shown. Press to mark the fold line.*

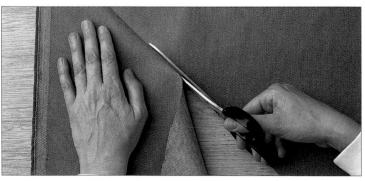

2 *Open out the fabric and cut carefully along the diagonal fold line. Use sharp scissors and keep as straight as possible.*

Sewing a Flat Seam

A flat seam is the simplest way to join two pieces of fabric. To keep seam allowances even and seams straight, align the raw edges of the fabric to the appropriate seam guidelines on your sewing machine.

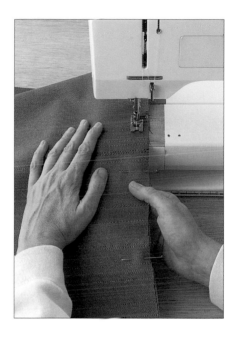

1 *With right sides together, pin the fabric with raw edges together. Machine stitch, leaving a 1.5cm (⅝ in) seam allowance. Backstitch at the start and finish of the stitching to reinforce the seam.*

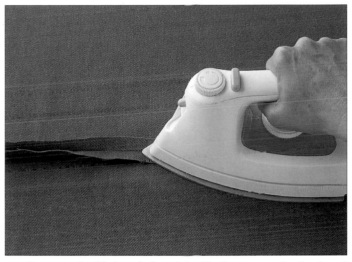

2 *Open out the fabric and place right side down on an ironing board or a flat surface suitable for ironing upon. Using the tip of the iron, press the seam flat.*

Finishing Raw Edges

The raw edges of a flat seam may need to be finished in some way to minimise fraying, particularly if the seam will be subject to strain or frequent washing. Here are two methods.

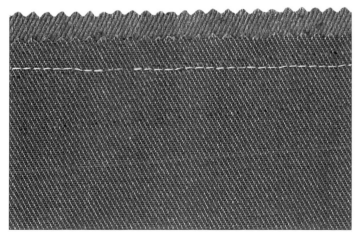

Pinking
Trim the raw edges of the seam with pinking shears to reduce fraying. To reduce bulk when using thick fabric, you can trim one side closer to the line of stitching than the other.

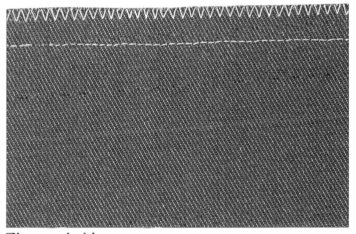

Zigzag stitching
Set the zigzag stitch on your machine to medium. Machine along the seam allowance, stitching close to but not on the raw edges. You can stitch both edges together as here or zigzag single layers.

133

French Seam

This is an enclosed seam in which the raw edges are
sewn into the finished seam. It creates a neat finish, which is particularly
useful for unlined items such as curtains or bedspreads.

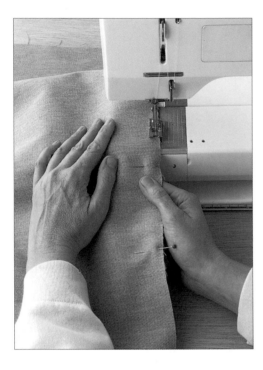

1 *With wrong sides together, pin the pieces of fabric together and machine stitch 5mm (¼in) from the raw edges.*

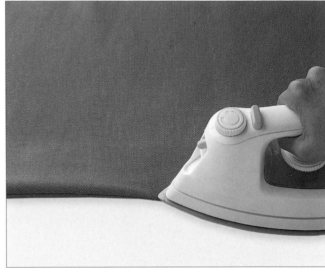

2 *Open out the fabric and press the seam open. Fold the fabric right sides together and press so that the seam is exactly on the folded edge.*

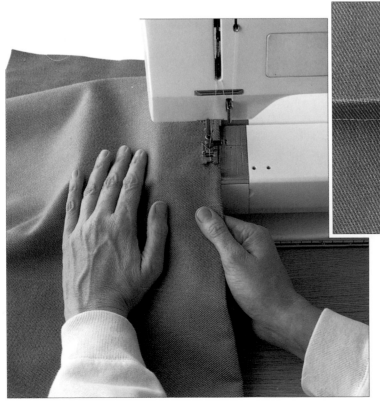

3 *On the wrong side, machine stitch 1cm (½in) from the fold line. When the seam is completed, the raw edges are neatly enclosed on the wrong side (see inset). Press the seam to one side on the wrong side so that it lies flat.*

Satin Stitch

A decorative machine stitch used for applying appliqué or for
effect. Practice on a scrap of fabric before trying satin stitch on your finished work.
You need a swing needle machine with a zigzag facility for this stitch.

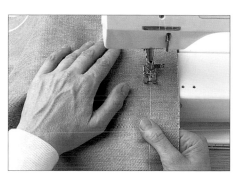

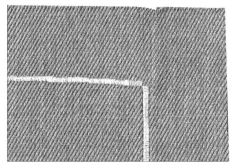

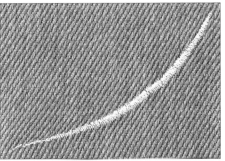

*1 With the stitch length set on long, do a
guideline of machine stitching to follow.
(For appliqué, simply follow the line of the
piece of fabric you are attaching.) Set your
machine to satin stitch, with a medium stitch
width and the stitch length just above zero.
Align the centre of the machine foot with the
guideline and satin stitch along the line.*

*2 To satin stitch around a corner, stop
when you reach the corner, lift the needle
and the foot and pivot the work 90 degrees.
Put the foot back down and continue
stitching in the new direction.*

*3 For tapering satin stitch (useful in
appliqué), start with the stitch length set
just below zero and the stitch width at zero.
Hold the work steady with your left hand,
keeping the right hand free to adjust the
stitch width. Start machining and gradually
adjust the stitch width control slowly and
smoothly up to a medium width in the centre
of the piece of stitching and back down to
zero again at the end.*

How to Keep Machine Stitching Straight

When you are stitching further than usual from the edge of the
fabric, place a piece of masking tape on the machine to help you align the fabric
and keep your line of stitching perfectly straight.

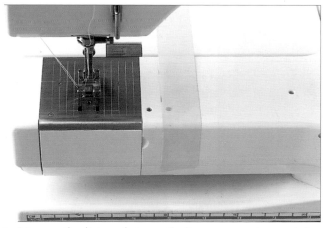

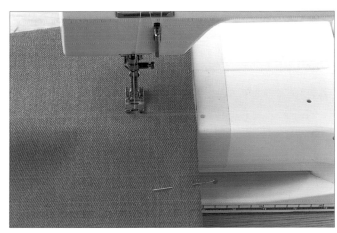

*1 Measure the distance between the line you are going to stitch
and the edge of the fabric. Measure this same distance from the
needle out to the right and mark with a piece of masking tape.*

*2 Place the fabric so that the edge aligns with the inside
of the masking tape. This will help you keep your line of
machine stitching straight.*

CURTAINS AND BLINDS

When working with the large expanses of fabric needed for curtains, it is best to have a work surface where you can spread the fabric out flat. This will help to ensure that you cut the fabric absolutely straight so that the finished item hangs correctly. Always double check your measurements before you start making up the project – there is nothing worse than finding your carefully stitched curtain or blind is too short for the window.

Making a Basic Curtain

Cut lining 10cm (4in) longer than the finished length and 4cm (1½in) narrower than the finished width (before pleating or gathering). See page 128 for information on how to measure your window and estimate fabric.

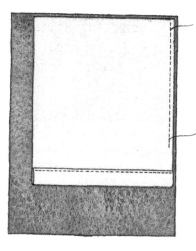

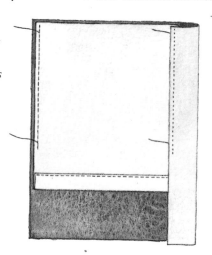

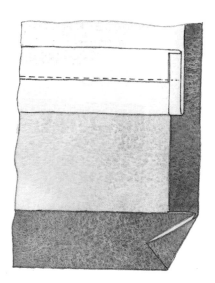

1 *Turn over a 5cm (2in) double hem on the lining and press. Machine stitch the hem in place. With right sides together and the top and one side edge aligned, pin lining to the main fabric, 1.5cm (⅝in) from top of curtain down to about 10cm (4in) above the lining hem. Machine stitch and press seam towards the lining.*

2 *Pull the lining over to align with the other side of the curtain fabric. Pin the sides together. Machine stitch the lining and main fabric together, leaving a 1.5cm (⅝in) seam allowance, down to about 10cm (4in) above the lining hem. Press seam towards the lining.*

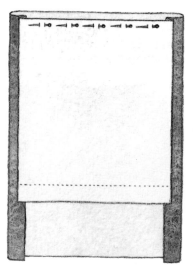

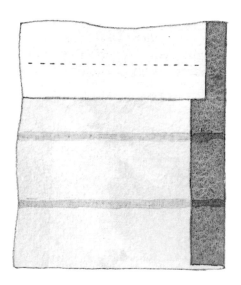

3 *Turn the curtain the right way out and centre the lining so that curtain side hems are both same width – 3.5cm (1½in). Pin across the top of curtain and lining to hold them in place.*

4 *Fold over 20cm (8in) at the base of the curtain fabric and press. Open out the fabric and fold the raw edge up to meet the 20cm (8in) fold line. Press.*

5 *Fold the hem up along the lower fold line. Mitre the corner of curtain by turning corner in diagonally 5cm (2in).*

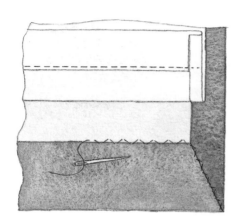

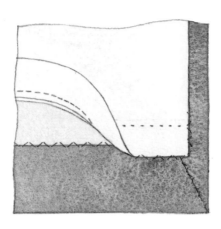

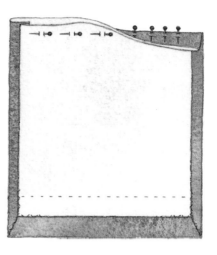

6 *Fold hem over again along the upper fold line. Sew mitres and hem in place by hand, using even slipstitch (see p.138).*

7 *Slipstitch the lining to the curtain from the end of the machine stitching and 5cm (2in) around corner. Finish securely. Repeat at the opposite corner.*

8 *Measure up from base of curtain several times across the width and mark the finished length along the top of the curtain with pins. Fold top of curtain down along pinned line and press. Remove crossways pins and re-pin vertically to hold fold.*

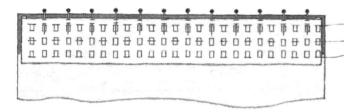

9 *Take a length of curtain tape and knot the strings together at the leading end of tape. Fold the tape under 1.5cm (⅝in). Pin the tape level with the top of the curtain, aligning the folded end with leading edge. At the other end of tape, pull strings free and fold under the end of the tape 1.5cm (⅝in) so that the folded edge is aligned with edge of curtain.*

10 *Start machine stitching at the top left-hand corner of tape. Backstitch to secure at the beginning, then machine along the top of the tape close to the edge. Backstitch at the end. Stitch the bottom of the tape to the curtain in the same way.*

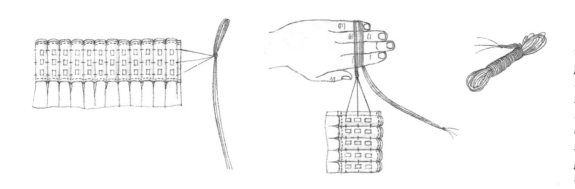

11 *Pull up the curtain strings until the gathered width equals the width of your pole or track (not forgetting returns and overlaps). Knot the strings with a slip knot, pulling the loop of the knot through about 7.5cm (3in). To keep the strings neat, make a 'sausage' by putting your fingers through the loop and winding the rest of the strings around them. Tuck the sausage under the strings in a fold of a pleat on the tape.*

Attaching Velcro to a Pelmet

A pelmet shelf should be between 10 and 20cm (4–8in) deep,
depending on the fullness of the curtains hung below. It is fixed to the wall
above the window with right-angled shelf brackets.

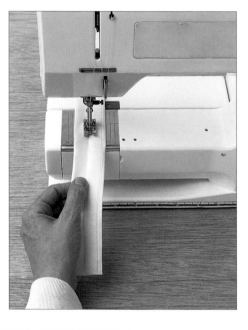

1 *Take a strip of lining fabric measuring the length of the finished pelmet (including returns) plus 3cm (1¼in), by the depth of the curtain tape plus 3cm (1¼in). Turn over 1.5cm (⅝in) at the top and bottom edges of the strip and press. Turn over 1.5cm (⅝in) at each end and press.*

2 *Take the soft side of the velcro and machine stitch to the top half of the right side of the lining strip, staying close to the top edge. Machine the bottom edge of the velcro and trim off any excess at the end.*

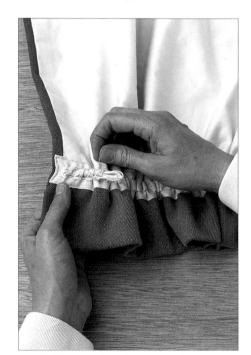

3 *Pull up the threads on the pelmet tape to gather it to the required width, making sure that gathers are evenly spaced. Make a slip knot in the threads and wind them into a neat bundle. Stitch the bundle to the tape.*

4 *Using slipstitch (see p. 138), hand sew the lining strip with the velcro facing outwards over the gathered tape. Stitch top and bottom, working over the gathers.*

5 *Take the pelmet shelf and staple the hard side of the velcro to the front and side edges of the shelf.*

Attaching Velcro to the Top of a Blind

A roman blind can be attached to a supporting lath with velcro.
The soft side of a velcro strip is sewn to the top of the blind. The hard side is stapled to
a lath, which is then screwed on or above the window frame.

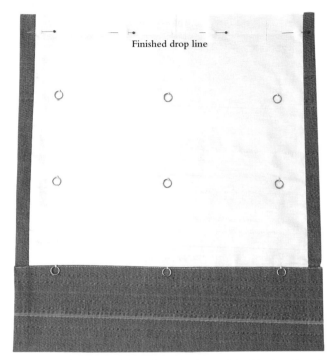

Finished drop line

1 *Measure the finished drop from the base of the blind and mark with a line of pins. Fold over at the marked line and press.*

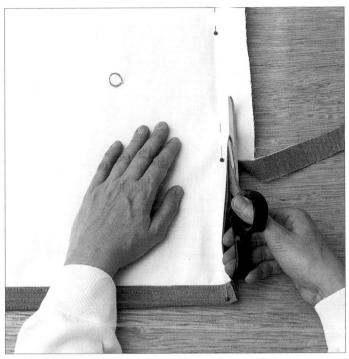

2 *Carefully trim away any excess fabric above the finished drop line, leaving a hem of about 1cm (½in).*

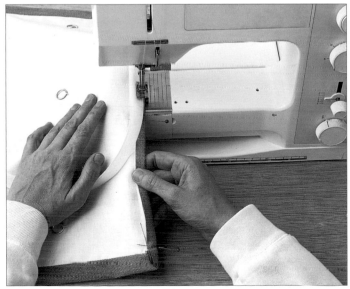

3 *Machine stitch the soft side of the velcro over the top hem. Keep very close to the top folded edge of the hem and remove pins as you reach them. Backstitch at the start and finish of the line of machine stitching.*

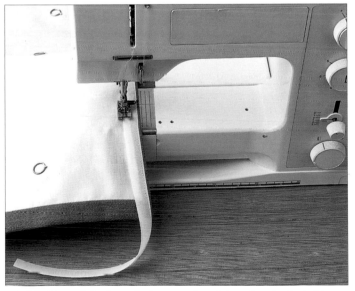

4 *Machine stitch along the bottom edge of the velcro, backstitching at the start and finish as before. Trim off any excess velcro.*

Covering a Lath for a Blind

For a neat coordinated finish, the lath for a blind should be wrapped in
the blind fabric before attaching velcro and screw eyes. The lath can then be fixed to the
wall or window frame using 4cm (1½in) right-angled brackets.

1 *Take a piece of standard 5 x 2.5cm (2 x 1in) wooden lath of the required width of the blind. Cut a length of fabric 15cm (6in) wide by the length of the lath plus 5cm (2in). Wrap the fabric around the wood and staple one side. Wrap the other side round and staple in place.*

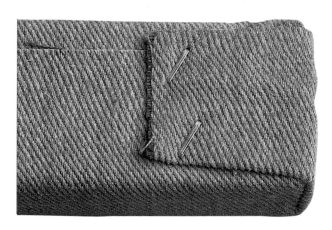

2 *Fold the ends over neatly as though wrapping a parcel and staple in place. If the fabric is thick, cut away some of the excess fabric underneath before stapling.*

3 *Using a staple gun, staple the hard side of the velcro to the front edge of the lath. Insert enough staples to hold the velcro securely.*

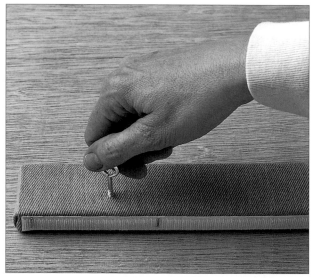

4 *Position screw eyes in line with the cords on the blind and 1.5cm (⅝in) from the front edge. Position an extra screw eye 2cm (¾in) from the end of the lath at the side where the cords will hang down – usually the right. Use a bradawl to make a hole through the fabric and into the wood and then insert screw eyes.*

144

Cording a Blind

A roman blind is raised and lowered by a cording system.
The cords run through the vertical rows of rings sewn to the back of the
blind and then through screw eyes on the fixing lath.

There are usually three cords running through three rows of rings on a roman blind. One row is set 10cm (4in) in from the right-hand edge of the blind, another is 10cm (4in) from the left-hand edge of the blind and the third runs up the centre. A screw eye is fixed to the underside of the fixing lath above each row of rings and an extra screw eye is placed 2cm (¾in) from the end of the lath at the side where the cords will hang down – usually the right. If the blind is wider than about 120cm (48in), you might want to add another row of rings so that there are four cords.

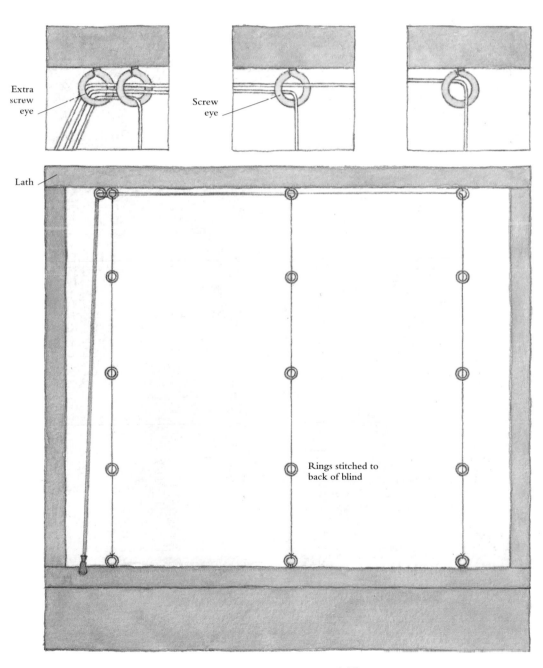

Extra screw eye

Screw eye

Lath

Rings stitched to back of blind

1 *Cut three lengths of cord roughly 2½ times the length of the blind. String up the blind by tying a cord to each of the bottom rings and threading it through all the rings above it.*

2 *Attach the blind to the lath (see p.143) and pass each cord through the screw eye directly above it and across through the other screw eyes, including the extra one at the end of the lath.*

3 *Thread all the cord ends through a cord weight or acorn and check that the blind is pulling up level. Knot the cords together below the acorn and cut off any surplus. Attach a cleat or hook to the wall or window frame. When the blind is raised, wind the cords around the cleat to hold it.*

FINISHING TECHNIQUES

Small details, such as neatly made buttonholes on a cushion cover, bias-cut piping round a bedhead or a matching stiffened tie-back on a door curtain, can make all the difference to home-made soft furnishings. These simple but effective finishing techniques all feature in the projects but are also useful for other items you might wish to make. Don't be tempted to rush these final touches – that little bit of extra effort will be sure to pay off.

Straight Tie

Ties made from fabric cut on the straight grain of fabric are ideal where the tie does not need to be very flexible. This style could be used for the loosely knotted ties that hold a blind or to fasten a cushion cover.

1 *Cut a piece of fabric twice the width of the finished tie plus 1cm (½in) seam allowance. Press over 5mm (¼in) to the wrong side along each long side of the fabric.*

2 *Fold the tie in half lengthways with the folded edges together and press.*

3 *At one end of the tie, fold in the raw edges 5mm (¼in). Machine stitch across this end and along the long side, keeping close to the folded edge. Leave the other end open. The raw edges will be concealed when the tie is attached to the item.*

Stitching on a Tie

This method of attaching a tie with a rectangle of stitching ensures that the tie is firmly secured. The method can be used to attach straight or bias-cut ties or ties made of tape or ribbon.

1 *Tuck under the raw edges of the tie and pin it in position. Start machine stitching at the top left corner, backstitching to secure. Stitch down the left side of the tie, counting stitches so that you can make the same amount on the other side. With the needle in the work, lift the foot and pivot the work. Lower the foot.*

2 *Machine stitch along the bottom of the rectangle. Lift the foot and pivot the work again. Lower the foot.*

3 *Machine stitch up the right-hand side of the rectangle, checking that you make the same number of stitches as on the left side. Pivot the work again.*

4 *Machine stitch across the top of the rectangle.*

5 *Machine stitch diagonally across the rectangle from top left to bottom right. Finally stitch up the right-hand side again to secure.*

Cutting and Joining Bias Strips

Fabric cut on the bias instead of the straight grain
has more 'give', so use bias-cut strips to cover piping cord and to make
ties that require flexibility.

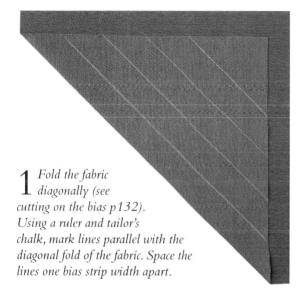

1 *Fold the fabric
diagonally (see
cutting on the bias p132).
Using a ruler and tailor's
chalk, mark lines parallel with the
diagonal fold of the fabric. Space the
lines one bias strip width apart.*

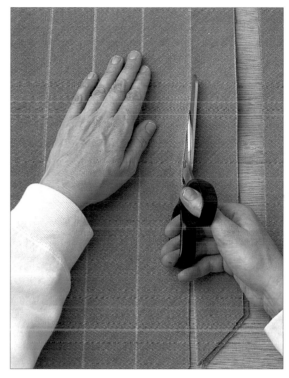

2 *Cut along the
folded diagonal line
and along all the
subsequent chalk lines.
Use sharp scissors and
cut the fabric as straight
as possible.*

3 *To join the strips, pin the ends of two strips with
right sides together so that they form a right angle.
Machine stitch 1cm (½in) from the ends.*

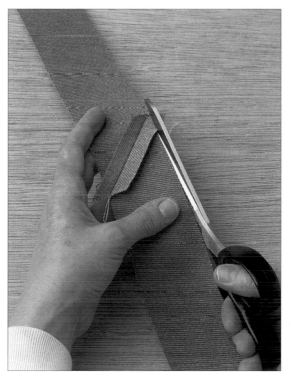

4 *Press the seam
open. To finish
the bias strips, trim
off excess fabric from
the corners.*

Making Buttonholes

Buttonholes are straightforward to make using a sewing machine. If your
sewing machine has a special buttonhole setting, follow the manufacturer's instructions.
Otherwise, use the satin stitching setting and follow the steps below.

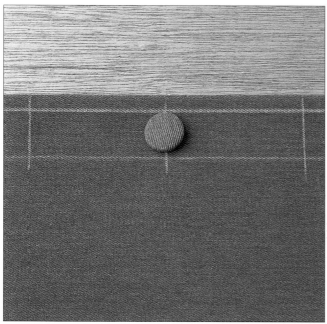

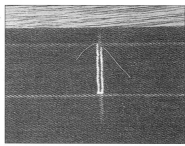

2 *With the needle to the left of the centre line, stitch down one side of the buttonhole. Leave the needle in the work, raise the foot and pivot the work 180°. Take one stitch towards the outer edge. Adjust the stitch width to its widest and take six stitches to form a bar tack at one end.*

3 *Adjust the stitch width back to just below medium and stitch down the other side of the centre line.*

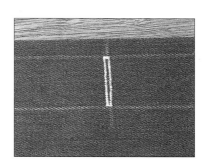

1 *Mark the width of the buttons you are going to use on the fabric with two parallel lines in tailor's chalk. Mark the positions of the buttonholes with vertical lines, which should be the diameter of the button plus 5mm (¼in). Set the stitch length on the sewing machine to just above zero and the stitch width to just below medium.*

4 *With the needle in the outer, left-hand side position, adjust the stitch width to its widest again. Stitch six stitches to make a bar tack. Adjust the stitch width to zero and take a few stitches to finish off securely. Take threads to the back and finish off securely.*

5 *Insert a stitch ripper or the blade of a small, very sharp pair of scissors and cut the buttonhole open, being careful not to slice through the bar tack.*

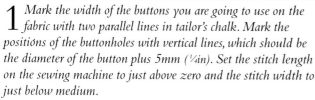

Inserting a Zip

This is a simple, straightforward method of inserting a zip fastener
into the seamline of, for example, a plain cushion cover. Make sure when you choose
a zip that it is suitable for the project style and fabric weight.

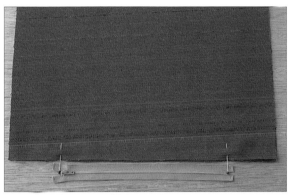

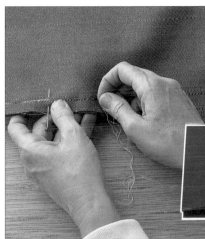

2 *Machine stitch to the beginning of the opening and backstitch to secure. Machine stitch the other side of the zip, backstitching to secure. Hand sew across the opening with large tacking stitches (see p. 138). Press the seam open (see inset).*

1 *Place the pieces of fabric right sides together. Centre the zip on the fabric and mark its length – from one stop to the other – with pins.*

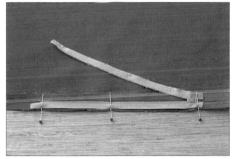

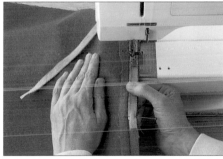

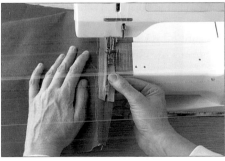

3 *Open the zip. Place face down on the extended seam allowance of the opening, lining up the stop with the end of the opening. Pin one side of the zip to the seam allowance with the teeth right on the seam.*

4 *With the zip foot on the machine and the needle to the left of the foot, machine stitch right from the start of the zip, keeping close to the teeth. Backstitch at the beginning and end to secure.*

5 *Turn the work round and extend the other seam allowance. Close the zip and machine stitch down the other side of the zip, again keeping the teeth close to the centre of the seam.*

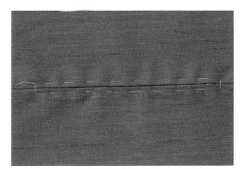

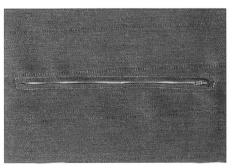

6 *Turn to the right side of the work. Using tacking stitches (see p. 138), sew round the top and bottom and both sides of the zip keeping 7mm (⅓in) from the centre seam.*

7 *Using the zip foot and with the needle on the left-hand side of the foot, machine stitch over the line of hand stitching, working down one side, across the top, down the other side and across the bottom.*

8 *Remove all the tacking stitches for the topstitching and from the centre seam.*

Making a Tassel from a Skein of Silk

Use a skein of embroidery silk to make this pretty
decorative tassel. Leave the paper bands in place while you make
the skein to keep all the strands together.

1 *Pull about 20cm (8in) or so from the skein and separate out two strands of silk. Fold these in half and put the looped end through the top of the skein. Pass the loose ends through the loop and pull tight.*

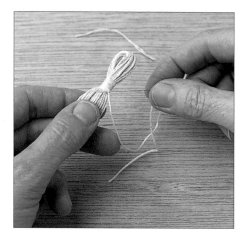

2 *Take a length of three or four strands of contrasting silk. Thread this onto a needle and wind it round and round the skein about 1.5cm (¾in) from the top, binding in the loose end. When the skein is tightly bound, sew in the end of the thread.*

3 *Take off the paper bands and cut the end of the skein to release the strands. Trim to even off the ends. Comb through the tassel with a fork to fluff it out (see inset). To attach the tassel, thread the loose thread at the top of the tassel onto a needle. Stitch the tassel securely in place.*

The wide range of colours available in embroidery thread means that you should have no trouble finding exactly the right shade to complement your fabric.

Making a Tassel from Wool or String

Any thread, from wool to garden twine, can be used to
make this decorative tassel, which makes an attractive finishing
touch for a bolster cushion.

1 *Cut a piece of card the width of the required length of the tassel. Wind the thread round the card to the thickness you want. Take a separate length of thread and place it through one end. Tie to secure the tassel.*

2 *Thread a needle with a length of contrasting thread and wind it round and round the tassel about 1.5cm (¼in) from the top. Bind in the loose end at the start and sew in the other end when you finish.*

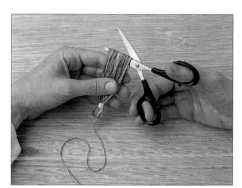

3 *Cut through the loops at the end of the tassel and trim if necessary.*

4 *Tease out the finished tassel with the end of a pin to give it fullness. Attach as for silk tassel.*

Quilt Embellishment

This fabric disk, attached with a french knot, is a quick and easy
way of adding decoration to a quilt. Since the edges of the fabric are simply pinked,
use something that does not fray too easily.

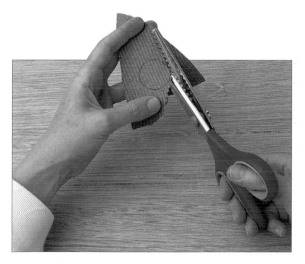

1 *You can use small scraps of fabric to make these discs. Draw round something of the required diameter, such as a coin. Cut the disc out with a pair of pinking shears.*

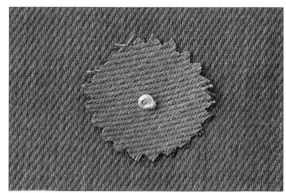

2 *Place on the quilt in the marked position and attach with a french knot (see p.139) in the centre of the disc.*

PAINT TECHNIQUES

EQUIPMENT

You do not need a huge range of equipment for the decorating projects in this book, but you do need the right tools for the job if you want good results. Successful dragging for example, is hard to achieve without a dragging brush. Always check what equipment you need and gather it all together. Otherwise you will reach a crucial stage and find that you need adhesive or a special brush.

When painting a room you will also need a ladder for reaching the ceiling and the tops of the walls, and a dust sheet for covering the floor and any furnishings.

Basics

Kettles and paint trays

Most foam rollers come complete with paint trays. Use the ridged area of the tray for removing excess paint from the roller before painting. When painting with a brush, pour paint into a paint kettle to make the job easier. Keep a roll of mutton cloth handy for tasks such as cleaning excess paint off your brush.

Squeegee

A rubber-edged squeegee is used to apply grout to tiles. The rubber pushes the grout between the tiles without damaging them.

Protective mask

A protective mask is an essential piece of equipment. It prevents the wearer breathing in dust particles and fumes which may be harmful.

Small paint tray and roller

Large paint tray and roller

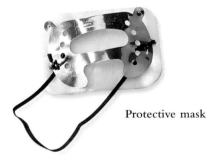

Protective mask

Kettles

Mutton cloth

Mask pads

Squeegee

160

Brushes

Basic brushes

Brushes are expensive, but try to equip yourself with at least a 10cm (4in) brush for applying paint to walls and 2.5cm (1in) and 5cm (2in) brushes for working on smaller areas, such as skirting boards and details. Buy the best quality you can afford – they will last longer and shed fewer hairs while you work.

2.5cm (1in) brush

5cm (2in) brush

10cm (4in) brush

Specialist brushes

You won't need all these brushes – only those for the techniques you want to try. Stippling brushes are available in a range of sizes. The larger the area you are stippling, the bigger brush you will need. An artist's brush is useful for adding small details. A badger brush is used for softening glaze in techniques such as marbling.

15cm (6in) brush for colourwashing

Dragging brush

Flogging brush

Badger brush

Large stippling brush

Small stippling brush

Stencil brush

Artist's brush

161

Preparation

Rubbing down and filling

Basic equipment for preparing surfaces before painting includes steel wool, a range of different grades of sandpaper, a filling knife and filler. A dusting brush for wiping surfaces free of dust and a wire brush for cleaning paint brushes are also useful. You will also need a ladder and a dust sheet for covering the floor and any furniture.

Sandpaper

Steel wool

Filler

Filling knife

Wire brush

Dusting brush

Measuring, Cutting and Sticking

Ruler and spirit level
A good steel ruler is essential for measuring and marking your wall for projects such as stripes. A spirit level is invaluable for checking that horizontal and vertical lines are straight. You will also need a pencil to mark lines.

Scissors and craftknife
Sharp scissors and a craft knife will be needed for stencilling and découpage and a special mat makes the task easier.

Tapes and glues
Make sure you have low-tack masking tape for masking stripes and attaching stencils and PVA adhesive for découpage.

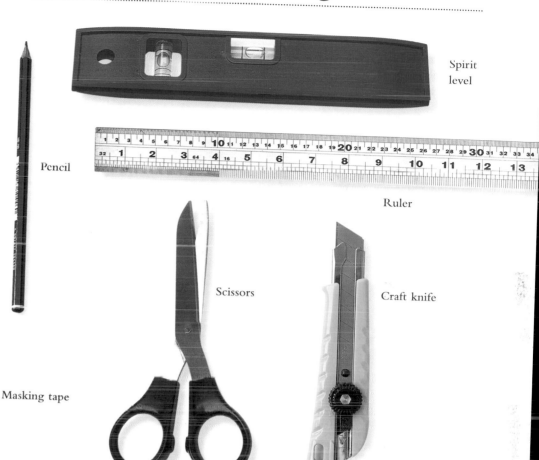

Spirit level

Pencil

Ruler

Scissors

Craft knife

Cutting mat

Masking tape

PVA glue, in plastic bottle or tin

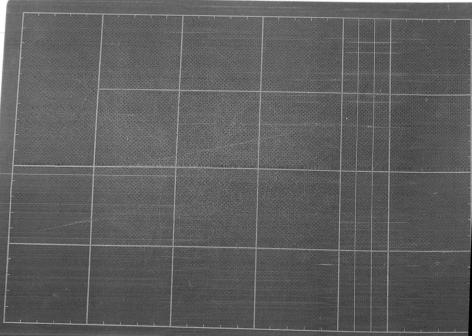

Working round obstacle
In every room stripes or checks will meet windows, doors and other obstacles. Don't worry about these. Just let the lines continue as they fall down or run across the wall. The finished effect will look all the more natural.

Never
enormo
quickes
wall has
is easy t

Marking Stone Blocks

Make sure that the size of the blocks is related to the size of the wall or room.
For a wall that is 2.5m (8ft) high, for example, blocks of 30cm (12in) deep and 60cm (24in) wide look good. The higher the room, the larger the blocks should be.

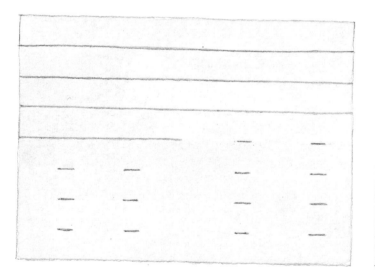

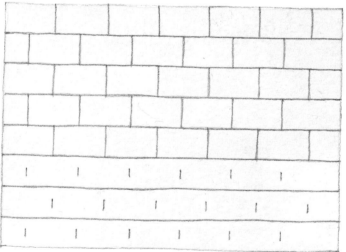

1 *Divide the wall into equal 30cm (12in) spaces and mark with pencil as shown. Make several marks at intervals across the wall. Using the marks as a guide, draw lines right across the wall with a spirit level or ruler. Starting from the top right corner of the wall, mark the width of the blocks at 60cm (24in) intervals. Don't worry if they are slightly smaller at the corners.*

2 *Draw in the vertical lines for the top row of blocks with a ruler or straight edge. Use this as a guide for the remaining blocks. The second line should be staggered as shown, so start with a half block. The third line should be the same as the first and so on.*

Marking Trompe L'oeil Panels

Trompe l'oeil panels can be made on walls or flat doors. A long wall looks best broken into three panels. On a shorter wall, make two panels of equal size. The panels here measure 60 x 80cm (24 x 32in), with 30cm (12in) in between each panel, but you can adapt the size to suit your wall.

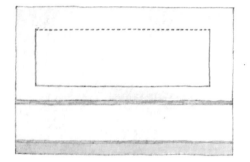 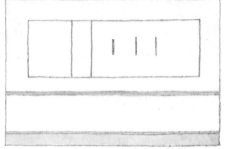 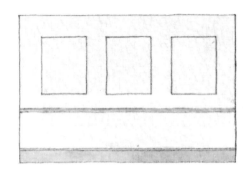

1 *Work out the total area of the panels from top to bottom and from the outside edge of the right-hand panel to the outside edge of the panel on the left. Centre this area on your wall about 10cm (4in) up from the dado and mark in pencil.*

2 *Mark the centre point of the centre panel. Mark the sides of the centre panel. Mark the inside edges of the left and right panels and draw in vertical lines. Use a spirit level to check your lines are straight.*

3 *Remove the line at the centre of the panels and the horizontal marks between the panels. The panels are now ready for painting (see p. 36).*

Marking a Wall for Stamping

Decide on how much space you want between each stamp on the wall. Bear in mind that if the stamps are too close together the wall will look very busy. Here the stamps are 60cm (24in) apart and the horizontal rows are 80cm (32in) apart.

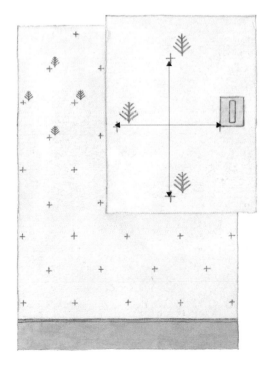

Mark the position of each stamp very lightly in pencil on the wall with a cross. Stagger the horizontal rows as shown so that each stamp in the second row comes halfway between two in the first row and so on. When stamping the wall, place the bottom left corner of the stamp in the angle of the cross marking the position. This will ensure that stamps are evenly positioned.

TEMPLATES AND STENCILS

The templates shown here are for use with the projects in the first part of this book. All are simple shapes, easy to trace or copy. If you want to make any of the templates bigger or smaller than illustrated, you can enlarge or reduce them on a photocopier or by copying them on to squared paper. You may, for example, prefer to use a smaller version of the heart shape for gilding or to appliqué a series of diamond shapes on to your bedlinen. The stencils shown on pages 183–185 are not the exact designs used in the projects, but provide you with a range of attractive ideas for use in your home.

Umbrella Stand Template

This diamond template is used for the gilded umbrella stand (see pp.20–21). Simple shapes like this work best with such a glamorous technique. To use the design at this size, simply trace over it, attach the design to the item and go over the line with pencil to transfer the outline to the wood.

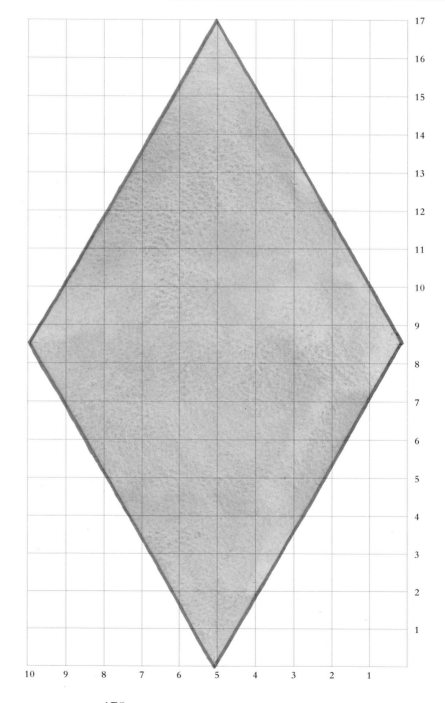

Pelmet Template

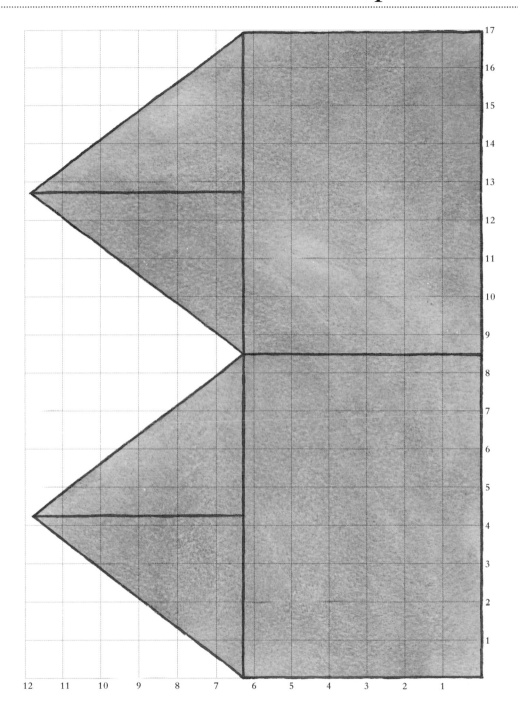

Each section of this template should be 15cm (6in) wide to fit the width of a finished panel of the pelmet (see pp.64–65). Photocopy the template, enlarging it by 75%. Attach the template to a piece of card and cut round it or trace the design on to the card. The card is then used to cut the pelmet to shape.

Topiary Templates

These simple templates help you make the spectacular mural on pp.88–89. You will need to enlarge the templates on a photocopier to make them big enough. Copy them in several sections onto A3 paper to make a finished image of about 80cm (32in) high. Then follow the instructions on p.89.

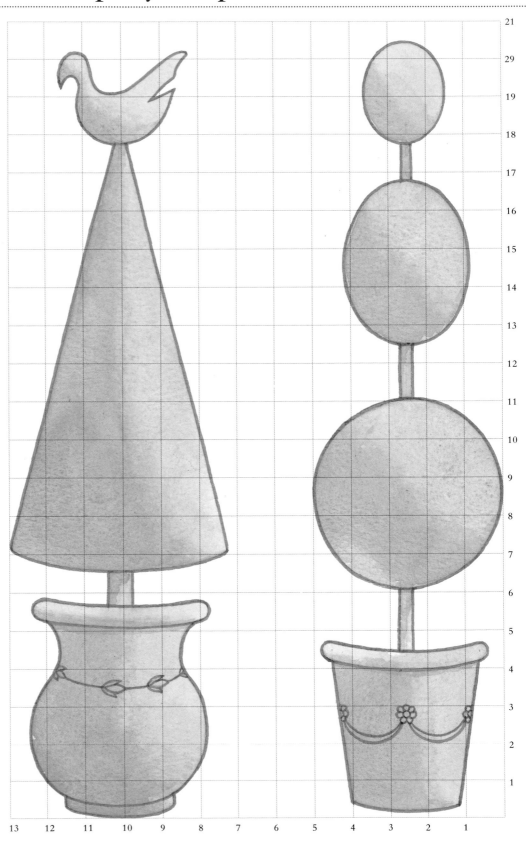

182

Bedroom Stencils

These stencil designs can be used to create the bedroom wall border on pp.96–97. To use any of these designs, trace the shape, working round all the shaded areas. Transfer the outline tracing to stencil card or acetate, shading the blocks to guide you as you cut. Carefully cut out all the shaded areas, keeping the areas in between them intact. For more details see p.172.

INDEX

SUPPLIERS

Fabric

Cath Kidston
115 Clarendon Road
London W11 4JG
Tel: 020 7229 8000

Designers Guild
for stockists tel 020 7243 7300

Henry Bertrand
Unit 3/21-22
Chelsea Harbour Design Centre
London SW10 0XE
For stockists tel 020 7349 1477

Ian Mankin
109 Regents Park Road
London NW1 8UR
020 7722 0997
Mail order catalogue available

James Brindley of Harrogate
Grafton House
Hookstone Park
Harrogate
North Yorkshire HG2 7DB
Tel: 01423 880400

Mulberry Design Company
Kilver Court
Shepton Mallet
Somerset BA4 5NF
For stockists tel 01749 340500

Osborne and Little
304 King's Road
London SW3 5UH
For stockists tel 020 7675 2255

Otillie Stevenson
101 Bethnal Green Road
London E2 7DG
For stockists tel 020 7739 9321

Romo Fabric
Lowmoor Road
Kirkby-in-Ashfield
Nottinghamshire
NG17 7DE
Tel: 01623 756699

Blank Furniture

Harvey Baker Design Ltd
Unit 1
Rodgers Industrial Estate
Yalberton Road,
Paignton, Devon TQ4 7PJ
Tel: 01803 521515

Scumble Goosie
Toadsmoor Road
Stroud,
Gloucestershire
GL5 2TB
Tel: 01453 731305

Paints

Annie Sloan Paints
Mail order from her on-line shop at
www.anniesloan.com or telephone
0870 601 0082

Askew Paint Centre
103 Askew Road
London W12 9RA
Tel: 020 8743 6612

Crown Paints
For details of paints and stockists
tel 01254 704951

Dulux Paints
For details of paints and stockists
tel 01753 556979

Farrow and Ball
Uddens Trading Estate
Wimborne
Dorset BH21 7NL
Tel: 01202 876141

Paper and Paints
4 Park Road
London SW10 0AD
Tel: 020 7352 8626

Mosaic

Edgar Udney & Co Ltd
314 Balham High Road
London SW17 7AA
Tel: 020 7767 8181
Mail order available

Fred Aldous
PO Box 135
37 Lever Street
Manchester 1 M60 1UX
Tel: 0161 236 2477 (general enquiries)
0161 236 4224 (mail order)

The Mosaic Workshop
Unit B
443-449 Holloway Road
London N7 6LJ
Mail order tel: 020 7263 2997

Stencils

Stencil Craft
115 Boldmere Road
Boldmere
Sutton Coldfield
B73 5TU
Tel:0121 354 7070
website: hhyp//www.stencil.co.uk

The Painted Finish
Unit 6
Hatton Country World
Hatton
Warwich CV35 8XA
Tel: 01926 842376

The Stencil Shop
Eyham Hall Craft Centre,
Eyham, Hope Valley,
Derby S32 5QW
Tel: 01433 639001

ACKNOWLEDGMENTS

The publishers would like to thank the following companies for kindly supplying materials and items for use in photography for this book. MO indicates mail order available.

Antiques

The Antique Trader, The Millinery Works, 85–87 Southgate Road, London N1 3JS, UK. Tel: 020 7359 2019.
Chairworks 75–80 Chelsea Bridge Business Centre, 326–342 Queenstown Road, London SW8 4NE, UK. Tel: 020 7498 7611.
Compton Antiques 45 The Street, Compton, Surrey GU3 1EG, UK. Tel: 01483 810505.
The Long Room Tel: 020 8392 4966.
The Old Cinema 157 Tower Bridge Road, London SE1 3LW, UK. Tel: 020 7407 5371.
243 243 Wimbledon Park Road, London SW18 5RJ, UK. Tel: 020 8875 9606.

Fabric and paint

Anna French 343 King's Road, London SW3 5ES, UK. Tel: 020 7351 1126. MO
The Cloth Shop 290 Portobello Road, London W10 5TE, UK. Tel: 020 8968 6001.
The Decorative Fabrics Gallery 278–280 Brompton Road, London SW3 2AS, UK. Tel: 020 7589 4778.
Designers Guild 267–277 King's Road, London SW3 5EN, UK. Tel: 020 7243 7300. MO
Farrow & Ball 249 Fulham Road, London SW3 6HY, UK. For mail order tel: 01202 876141.
Fired Earth 117–119 Fulham Road, London SW3 6RL, UK. Tel: 020 7589 0489.
Jane Churchill for further details contact Farrow & Ball.
Leyland Paints from Nuline, 305–317 Westbourne Park Road, London W11 1EF, UK. Tel: 020 7727 7748. MO
Melin Tregwynt Tregwynt Mill, Castlemorris, Haverfordwest, Pembrokeshire, Wales SA62 5UX, UK. Tel: 01348 891644. MO
Mulberry Design Company Kilver Court, Shepton Mallet, Somerset, BA4 5NF, UK. Tel: 01749 340500.
Osborne & Little for stockists' details Tel: 020 7675 2255. MO
Paint Magic 48 Golborne Road, London W10 5PR, UK, for stockists' details tel: 020 8960 9960. MO
Ottilie Stevenson, 101 Bethnal Green Road, London E2 7DG, UK. Tel: 020 7739 7321.
Ruffle & Hook 122–124 St John Street, London EC1V 4JS, UK. Tel: 020 7490 4321.

Flooring

Amtico for stockists' details tel: 01203 861400. MO
Crucial Trading PO Box 11, Duke Place, Kidderminster,

Shropshire DY10 2JR, UK. Tel: 01562 820005.
Roger Oates Design 1 Monro Terrace, London SW10 0DL, UK. Tel: 020 7351 2288. MO
The Rug Company 103 Lots Road, London SW10 0RN, UK. For mail order tel: 020 7467 0690.
Stone Age 19–23 Filmer Road, Fulham, London SW6 7BU, UK. For brochure tel: 020 7385 7954.

Furniture

Angraves Cane Furniture for stockists' details tel: 0116 269 4321.
Acro 347–349 King's Road, London SW3 5ES, UK. Tel: 020 8971 0066 for mail order
alphabeds 92 Tottenham Court Road, London W1P 9HE, UK. Tel: 020 7636 6840
Freud 198 Shaftesbury Avenue, London WC2H 8JL, UK. Tel: 020 7831 1071. MO
Hitch Mylius Alma House, 301 Alma Road, Enfield, Middlesex EN3 7BB, UK. For suppliers' details tel: 020 8443 2616.
Interiors Bis 60 Sloane Avenue, London SW3 3DD, UK. Tel: 020 7838 1104, website: www.interiorsbis.com
Nordic Style 109 Lots Road, London SW10 0RN, UK. Tel: 020 7351 1755. MO
Purves & Purves 80–81, Tottenham Court Road, London W1P 9HD, UK, for brochure tel: 0870 603 0205.
Royal Arrow 12 Stratford Road, London W8 6QD, UK. For stockists' details tel: 020 7938 2000.
SCP 135–139 Curtain Road, London EC2A 3BX, UK. Tel: 020 7739 1869.
Shaker 72–73 Marylebone High Street, London W1M 3AR, UK. Tel: 020 7935 9461. MO
Soo San 239a Fulham Road, London SW3 6HY, UK. Tel: 020 7352 8980.

Home accessories

Acquisitions (Fireplaces) Ltd Acquisitions House, 24–26 Holmes Road, London NW5 3AB, UK. Tel: 020 7482 2949.
Agnes B 111 Fulham Road, London SW3 6RL, UK. Tel: 020 7225 3477.
Anthony Redmile 533 King's Road, London SW10 0TZ, UK. Tel: 020 7351 3813. MO
The Bradley Collection Lion Barn, Maitland Road, Needham Market, Suffolk IP6 8NS, UK. Tel: 01449 722724.
Christopher Wray Lighting 591–593 King's Road, London SW6 2YW, UK. Tel: 020 7736 8434, website: www.christopher-wray.com
Divertimenti Retail Ltd 45–47 Wigmore Street, London W1H 9LE, UK. Tel: 020 7935 0689.
Floris 89 Jermyn Street, London SW1Y 6JH, UK. Tel: 020 7930 2885. MO
Imperial Towel Rails for stockists' details tel: 01543 571615. MO

The Laundry PO BOX 22007, London SW2 1WU, UK.
Tel: 020 7274 3838.
Neal Street East 5 Neal Street, Covent Garden, London WC2H
9PU, UK. Tel: 020 7240 0135. MO
Neal's Yard Remedies 15 Neal's Yard, Covent Garden, London
WC2H 9DP, UK. For mail order tel: 0161 831 7875.
Nicole Farhi Home for further details tel: 020 7494 9051.
Ocean Home Shopping mail order only, tel: 0870 2426283,
website: www.oceancatalogue.com
The Pot Company 16–20 Raymouth Road, London SE16 2DB,
UK. Tel: 020 7394 9711.
Quintessa Art Collection, Palace of Industry, Engineers Way,
Wembley, Middlesex HA9 ODA, UK. Tel: 020 8795 3620.
Samuel Heath & Sons for stockists' details Tel: 0121 766 4200.
Toast for mail order tel: 01558 668800.
A Touch of Brass 210 Fulham Road, London SW10 9PJ, UK.
Tel: 020 7351 2255.
The White Company mail order only, tel: 020 7385 7988.

General stores

B&Q for branch details tel: 0500 300150.
Habitat for branch details tel: 0845 6010740.
Laura Ashley for branch details tel: 0990 622116.
John Lewis for branch details tel: 020 7629 7711.
Liberty Regent Street, London W1R 6AH, UK.
Tel: 020 7734 1234. MO
Sainsbury's Homebase for branch details tel: 0845 9801800
Wickes, for branch details tel: 0500 300328

Miscellaneous

Adolfo Dominguez, 57 South Molton Street, London W1Y 1HH,
UK. Tel: 020 7629 2571.
Ariel Crittall (artist) tel: 01371 810250.
Arthur Beale (chandlers) 194 Shaftesbury Avenue, London WC2H
8JP, UK. Tel: 020 7836 9034.
The Camden Garden Centre 2 Barker Drive, St Pancras Way,
London NW1 0JW, UK. Tel: 020 7485 8468.
David Armstrong Designs 152 Gray's Inn Road, London WC1X
8AX, UK. Tel: 020 7837 2667.
Emma Hope Shoes 53 Sloane Square London SW1 8AX, UK. Tel:
020 7259 9566.
James Smith & Sons Hazelwood House, 53 New Oxford Street,
London WC1A 1BL, UK. Tel: 020 7836 4731.
Soho Shoes, 93 Wimpole Street, London W1M 7DA, UK.
Tel: 020 7629 1888.
Wallace & Sewell for stockists' details tel: 020 7251 2143.
Wheatley's Flowers 33–34 Myddleton Street, London EC1R 1UA,
UK. Tel: 020 7278 6662.

Authors' Acknowledgments

Gina Moore would like to thank the following for kindly
supplying fabric:
Ian Mankin Contrast-lined Door Curtain, Café Curtain, Child's
Quilt, Lined Baskets, Bench Cushion, Bathroom Organiser.
Osborne and Little Console Table Cover, Director's Chair.
Romo Fabric Blind with Ties, Roman Blind, Cube Footstool,
Throw.
James Brindley of Harrogate Pleated Curtains with Pelmet.
Henry Bertrand Envelope Cushions.
Cath Kidston Table Napkins and Place Mats.
Otillie Stevenson Tie-on Seat Cushions, Bolster Cushion.
Designers Guild Bed Canopy, Bathroom Organiser.
Mulberry Roller Blind.

Amy Dawson would like thank the following for kindly supplying
paints and other materials:
Harvey Baker Design Ltd, The Mosaic Workshop, Annie Sloan
Paints, Askew Paint Centre, Paper and Paints, Farrow and Ball,
The Painted Finish

Gina and Amy would also like to thank Lucinda Symons, Brian
Hatton, Sam Lloyd and everyone at the studio, Ali Edney for great
style, Steve Gott for building the sets, everyone at C&B Packaging
particularly Helen Collins and last, but not least, our editor Jinny
Johnson for all her help and patience.